Instructor's Manual and Test Bank
to accompany

Earth Science
and the Environment

Second Edition

by Thompson & Turk

Christine Seashore

SAUNDERS GOLDEN SUNBURST SERIES

Saunders College Publishing
Harcourt Brace College Publishers

Fort Worth Philadelphia San Diego New York Orlando Austin
San Antonio Toronto Montreal London Sydney Tokyo

Printed in the United States of America

ISBN 0-03-021469-6

9 0 1 2 3 4 5 6 7 8 023 10 9 8 7 6 5 4

PREFACE

Earth Science encompasses geology, oceanography, meteorology, climatology, and astronomy: the sciences related to the Earth and other objects in the Universe. In <u>Earth Science and the Environmen</u> we teach the fundamentals of each of these subjects and, at the same time, use their respective concepts to explain their roles in the human environment and the effects of human activities on the natural world.

We feel that Earth Science comes to life for both professionals and students when its concepts are used to explain specific and familiar events and phenomena. Because of this orientation, we use familia examples and cite case studies throughout the book. We describe and explain basic concepts for each topic discussed in the text, and give them vitality and relevance by applying them immediately to specific examples. Whenever possible, we refer to places and events that are known to most students. In this way, we rely on and augment an existing familiarity and interest. This approach of applying general concepts to familiar places strongly reinforces the learning process and helps students maintain their interest in Earth Science long after the introductory course has ended.

Each of us who teaches Earth Science has developed his or her own ways of selecting, organizing, and presenting the topics of the course. Most of us do our best to capitalize on our own strengths. Fo these reasons, we do not believe that there is one best sequence for an introductory course, nor a particular way in which a topic should be presented. We do feel that this text presents topics in a logic order, and that information is presented so that it is useful as background for following chapters. However, other sequences are equally reasonable. Therefore, we have written the book so that individu chapters or groups of chapters can stand alone, and can be used in almost any sequence. Where information in a previous chapter is used in a later chapter, we refer the reader to the original discussion In this way, if a student needs to have his or her memory refreshed, or wants a quick introduction to a concept, he or she can find it quickly.

Each chapter in this manual is divided into four sections.

(1) **Discussion**: In this section we highlight topics in the text that we feel are most important or interesting. In some cases we add information that is relevant to the chapter, but is not included in the text. Some professors may wish to incorporate this information into lectures or classroom discussions. In some cases, alternative teaching sequences are suggested where we feel that they may be helpful.

(2) **Answers to Discussion Questions**: The discussion questions in the text are designed to be thought-provoking and to serve as springboards for classroom discussion. Answers are given for some, and in instances where there are no "correct" answers, we discuss plausible responses based on the concepts presented in the chapter. Answers to the review questions can be taken directly from the text of each chapter, so those answers are not repeated here.

(3) **Selected Reading**: A selected bibliography is provided as reference for additional lecture material, or to provide references to students for further research into the topics.

(4) **Test**: A test consisting of multiple choice, true or false, and completion questions is provided for each chapter. An answer key follows each chapter test for the instructor's convenience.

Instructor's Manual with Test Bank
To Accompany

Earth Science and the Environment 2nd Edition

TABLE OF CONTENTS

CHAPTER 1

Earth Systems

Discussion

We open the book with a brief introduction to the Earth's four realms -- the geosphere, hydrosphere, atmosphere, and biosphere, and then proceed to discussions of geologic time, and the formation and structure of the Earth.

The main focus of the second edition of Earth Science and the Environment is to teach fundamental Earth processes within a systems interaction framework. Thus a change in one realm, or one portion of a realm, can affect seemingly disparate parts of the whole. While people have understood the systems approach to Earth science for a long time, recent research has unearthed new relationships that were not even considered only a few decades ago. Many of the ideas that we discuss in this text appeared in the literature within the past few years. We refer frequently to the recent literature to teach students about the scientific process and to emphasize that science advances through ideas, discussion, disagreement, and development of models and hypotheses.

Perhaps one of the oldest questions in Earth science is, "How fast does change occur?" We discuss this issue in Chapter 1 because the answer affects student's understanding of many topics throughout the text. Whereas Earth scientists once argued the relative merits of gradualism versus uniformitarianism, we now understand that both models have operated frequently in the past; slow and rapid change have both altered the course of Earth history.

The literature contains many examples of situations where small initial perturbations have affected other components of the system, which amplified the original affect until a threshold was crossed. At the threshold, rapid and sometimes cataclysmic change occurred. We will discuss many examples of these processes throughout the text. However, the concept is so important and so integral to a systems approach to Earth Science, that we conclude the chapter with a brief introduction of feedback and threshold mechanisms.

Answers to Discussion Questions

1. Since fresh water is essential for life on land, and the usable water is limited, excess consumption and pollution threaten our well-being. In addition, small perturbations in geology, ecosystem distribution, or climate can cause large changes in the distribution of fresh water.

2. This question asks the student to think about topics that will be discussed throughout the

book. This question is answered in the Unit Opener essay to Unit VI. Internal processes originate deep within the Earth and aren't controlled by living organisms, whereas surface processes are influenced by people, plants, and animals. Agriculture and logging have altered a large portion of the continents. People profoundly affect fresh water on land (see answer to Discussion 1 above) and the atmosphere. In turn, changes in the hydrosphere and atmosphere affect the solid Earth and the remainder of the biosphere.

3. If the longest half-lives of the Earth's radioactive isotopes were a few million years, the Earth would have become molten soon after its formation. Nearly all of these short half-lived radioactive isotopes would have decomposed during the 4.6 billion years of the Earth's history, so today our planet would be cooler than it is now. Volcanism, earthquake activity, and tectonic motion would be less pronounced than it is today.

4. There are many possible examples for each statement. We offer two for each statement.

a. Changes in the solid Earth perturb the hydrosphere: Movement of the continents affects the distribution and direction of ocean currents. Tectonic uplift (mountain building) affects stream flow and precipitation.

b. Changes in the hydrosphere perturb the solid Earth: Ocean waves and currents shape coastlines by eroding, transporting, and depositing sediment. Streams and glaciers sculpt landforms also by eroding, transporting, and depositing sediment.

c. Changes in the solid Earth perturb the atmosphere: Volcanoes emits gases and particles that alter atmospheric composition. Mountains alter winds and precipitation patterns.

d. Changes in the atmosphere perturb the solid Earth: Because greenhouse gases absorb infrared heat, the Earth's temperature is partially controlled by atmospheric composition. In turn, temperature is an important component of climate, which affects the distribution of water and ice, and other factors that control erosion, transport, and deposition. The atmosphere also weathers rocks and minerals.

e. Changes in the solid Earth perturb the biosphere: Volcanic eruptions can alter climate, which affects living organisms. The height, extent, and distribution of mountains also affects climate and life on Earth.

f. Changes in the biosphere perturb the solid Earth: Plants help create and retain soil, thereby profoundly altering the Earth's surface. Humans alter the Earth's surface in many ways by altering plant cover for agriculture, paving urban areas, draining wetlands, altering stream flow, and many other activities.

g. Changes in the hydrosphere perturb the atmosphere: The hydrosphere is liquid water and water vapor is part of the atmosphere. Therefore, the hydrosphere and atmosphere are intimately linked. Any alteration in the distribution of surface water affects the atmosphere in many ways.

h. Changes in the atmosphere perturb the hydrosphere: The argument offered above works in reverse. If the air cools, less water will evaporate, rainfall and stream flow will diminish. Sufficient cooling may lead to growth of glaciers. Changes in the composition of the atmosphere -- amount of dust, cloud cover, or gaseous composition -- affect climate and therefore affect the hydrosphere.

i. Changes in the hydrosphere perturb the biosphere: Plant growth is dependent on soil moisture; a change in the hydrosphere can turn a desert into a rainforest or vice versa. Water also sculpts landforms which alter local climates; when glaciers and streams erode a high mountain range into a series of low hills, the local climate and plant cover changes.

j. Changes in the biosphere perturb the hydrosphere: A forest cools the air above it and promotes rainfall. Forest soils retain moisture. If a forest is cut the total rainfall decreases. Runoff increases dramatically during rainy times and decreases dramatically when it is not raining.

k. Changes in the atmosphere perturb the biosphere: Many examples can be used to illustrate that the atmosphere regulates climate; climate regulates life.

l. Changes in the biosphere perturb the atmosphere: Early in Earth history, photosynthetic organisms released enough oxygen into the atmosphere to change its composition (and to make multicellular life as we know it possible). Today, humans are increasing the carbon dioxide concentration of the atmosphere through industrial emissions.

5. In Earth science: Today, dense, cold salty water in the North Atlantic sinks, initiating a deep-ocean circulation that profoundly affects global climate. If this water becomes warmer or less salty, eventually it reaches a threshold where it is more buoyant than the deeper water. The moment the North Atlantic surface water stops sinking, both surface and deep water currents change. Abundant evidence shows that these changes not only change regional weather, but global climate.

In politics: For years after the Gulf War, Saddam Hussein interfered with the UN weapons inspectors in Iraq. However, when he took one additional step by barring inspection of his palaces, he challenged Clinton to the point where the US threatened military action.

In human relationships: Just think of an example where you have annoyed your girlfriend, boyfriend, parent, or roommate until one final additional action initiated a reprisal or argument. The final step may have seemed trivial but it was "the straw that broke the camel's back".

Selected Reading

Definitions as given throughout this text are from Robert L. Bates and Julia A. Jackson, eds., *Dictionary of Geological Terms*. Garden City, NY: Anchor Press, 1984.

A good introduction for students of Earth science is
Gerard V. Middleton and Peter R. Wilcock, *Mechanics in the Earth and Environmental Sciences*.
Cambridge: Cambridge University Press, 1994, 459 pages.

For a detailed look at the study of Earth's history
David Oldroyd, *Thinking About the Earth: A History of Ideas in Geology*. Boston: Harvard
University Press, 1996, 410 pages.

The importance of catastrophic events in Earth history is discussed in Derek Ager, *The New
Catastrophism: The Importance of the Rare Event in Geological History*. New York: Cambridge
University Press, 1993.

Early Earth is discussed in
John Gribbin and Mary Gribbin, *Fire on Earth: How Asteroid and Comet Collisions Have
Shaped Human History--And What Dangers Lie Ahead*. New York: St. Martin Griffin, 1997,
264 pages.

Harry Y. McSween Jr., *Fanfare for Earth: The Origin of Our Planet and Life*. New York: St.
Martin, 1997, 252 pages.

Tyler Volk, *Gaia's Body: Toward a Physiology of Earth*. New York: Copernicus Press, 1998.
269 pages.

George W. Wetherill, "Formation of the Earth," *Annual Review of Earth and Planetary Sciences*,
Volume 18, 1990.

More detail on the formation of the Solar System is offered by:
Andrew Fraknoi, David Morrison, and Sidney Wolff, *Voyages Through the Universe*,
Philadelphia: Saunders College Publishing, 1997, 595 pages.

Jay M. Pasachoff's text, *Astronomy: from Earth to the Universe, 5th ed.*, Philadelphia: Saunders
College Publishing, 1998, 643 pages.

Chapter 1 Test

Multiple Choice:

1. Deep ground water saturating rock a kilometer underground is a component of the
(a) atmosphere; (b) biosphere; (c) hydrosphere; (d) geosphere.

2. A pool of liquid magma is a component of the
(a) atmosphere; (b) biosphere; (c) hydrosphere; (d) geosphere.

3. Complex multicellular organisms have been abundant on our planet for about _____ percent of Earth history.
(a) 0.1; (b) 1.0; (c) 10; (d) 50

4. The planets in our Solar System formed
(a) when a fiery hot nebula in space coalesced under the force of gravity; (b) from huge meteoroids that had been flying through intergalactic space; (c) when the early Sun exploded, shooting rocky debris into space; (d) from a coalescing frigid cloud of dust and gas.

5. Geologists recently estimated that the Earth's core formed 62 million years after the Earth coalesced. This measurement supports the hypothesis that
(a) the Earth was originally homogeneous and later separated into a core and mantle; (b) the Earth's layers formed as the planet coalesced; (c) the core is composed of iron and nickel; (d) the mantle is composed of iron and nickel.

6. A tectonic plate is composed of
(a) cool, rigid rock that rides on a plastic mantle; (b) cool, rigid rock that rides on a continuous shell of molten magma; (c) hot, plastic rock supported by a rigid foundation of cool rock; (d) cool rigid rock that floats on the Earth's molten core.

7. Which of the following is a system?
(a) the human body; (b) the digestive organs in a human body; (c) a bacterium that lives within the small intestine; (d) all of the above

8. The two fundamental sources of energy that drive Earth systems are:
(a) the Sun and the wind; (b) the Sun and the Earth's interior heat; (c) meteorite impacts and the solar wind; (d) The Earth's interior heat and the wind.

9. Uniformitarianism states that:
(a) the Earth is uniform throughout its interior; (b) the Earth's mantle is uniform, although it is different from the crust and core; (c) catastrophic events such as volcanic eruptions alter the Earth; (d) geologic change occurs over long periods of time by a sequence of almost imperceptible events.

10. Imagine that a system has been perturbed at a constant rate for a long time, but the system has barely changed. Suddenly, a small additional perturbation causes a large change in the system. This scenario is an example of
(a) uniformitarianism; (b) catastrophism; (c) a threshold effect; a feedback mechanism.

True or False:

1. The hydrosphere includes water in streams, lakes, and oceans; in the atmosphere; and frozen in glaciers.

2. The Earth's atmosphere is a mixture of gases, mostly nitrogen and hydrogen.

3. The biosphere consists solely of the thin zone on the surface of the continents that is inhabited by life.

4. Below a thin layer of soil and beneath the ocean water, the outer layers of the Earth are composed entirely of molten rock.

5. The Earth's core is composed of hot, partially molten granite.

6. The earth's mantle lies over the core and the crust lies over the mantle.

7. More water exists in the earth's atmosphere than in surface streams and lakes.

8. Oceans cover about 71 percent of the Earth.

9. The Earth's atmosphere acts as a blanket, retaining heat at night and dispersing direct solar heating during the day.

10. The Earth is about 460 million years old.

Completion:

1. The geosphere consists of three major layers, the _____, the _____, and the _____

2. The _____ zone inhabited by life.

3. Oceans cover the planet and contain about _____ percent of its water.

4. The _____ is a mixture of gases, mostly nitrogen and oxygen.

5. During the formation of planets, gravitational forces caused small rocky spheres to collide and coalesce to form mini-planets, called _____.

6. The _____ of the Earth is a thin, rigid surface veneer that lies above the mantle.

7. The Earth's outer, cool, rigid shell is broken into several segments called _____.

8. The central portion of the Earth, called the _____, contains a solid layer surrounded by a liquid layer.

9. A _____ is any combination of interrelated, interacting components.

10. _____ is a principle that states that occasional huge catastrophes alter the course of Earth history.

11. A _____ _____ occurs when a small initial perturbation affects another component of the system, which amplifies the original effect.

12. A/an _____ is a tentative explanation of observations built on strong supporting evidence.

Answers for Chapter 1

Multiple Choice: 1. c; 2. d; 3.c; 4. d; 5. a; 6. a; 7. d; 8. b; 9. d; 10. c

True or False: 1.T; 2. F; 3. F; 4.F; 5.F; 6.T; 7.F; 8.T; 9.T; 10. F

Completion: 1. crust, mantle, core; 2. biosphere; 3. 97.5; 4. atmosphere; 5. planetesimals; 6. crust; 7. tectonic plates; 8. core; 9. system; 10. Catastrophism; 11. feedback mechanism; 12. hypothesis

CHAPTER 2

Minerals

Discussion

Chapters 2 and 3 discuss minerals and rocks, the materials that make up the solid Earth, or geosphere. We discuss both the nature of minerals and rocks and the processes by which they form and change.

At least two aspects of minerals commonly fascinate introductory geology students because they are familiar: crystals and gems. Class interest can be stimulated by pointing out that the striking crystal faces of diamonds and other gems results from the perfect ordering of atoms in the crystals, and that many gems are simply beautiful varieties of common minerals.

The knowledge that only a few minerals are common, and that they can be identified correctly with a bit of practice, is another aspect of the study of minerals that usually draws most students into the subject. It seems to give students a good feeling to know that only a few minerals are abundant, and therefore they can easily learn to identify most minerals in most rocks.

We begin Chapter 2 by pointing out that all rocks are made of one or more minerals. Therefore, minerals are the fundamental building blocks of the Earth. For this reason, an appreciation of the nature of minerals and a basic knowledge of the few, common, rock-forming minerals lays a foundation for the study of the Earth.

The chapter explains that the essential nature of a mineral is that it has a crystalline structure -- an orderly, repetitive, arrangement of atoms -- and a definite chemical composition. We then describe the physical properties of minerals and explain how these properties can be used to identify minerals. We stress the point, however, that the most important aspect of field identification is <u>recognition</u> of common minerals, aided by a few simple tests of physical properties. The common rock-forming minerals, along with a few examples of accessory minerals, gems, ore minerals, and industrial minerals, are then described.

Focus On boxes describe chemical bonding in minerals, and asbestos minerals and their carcinogenic properties.

Answers to Discussion Questions

1. Two properties differentiate one mineral from all others: chemical composition and crystal structure. If diamond and graphite are different minerals, but have identical chemical compositions, they must have different crystal structures. Diamond is cubic, and all carbon-

carbon bonds are strong covalent bonds. Graphite is hexagonal, and each carbon is bonded to three other carbons by similar covalent bonds, but to a forth carbon with a weak van der Waals bond. It is this weak bond that is responsible for the softness and cleavage of graphite, and for its properties of electrical conductance and opacity as well.

2. The discussion of this question depends on each student's familiarity with the elements. Most will at least be familiar with the names of the 8 most abundant elements. Other elements that are familiar, but less abundant, include hydrogen, gold, silver, other precious and industrial metals, carbon, sulfur, nitrogen, etc. Each is familiar because it is important to humans for industrial use, jewelry, or, as is the case with hydrogen, survival (as a component of water).

3. Silicon and oxygen combine to form the silicate tetrahedron. Since all of the Earth's silicon, and most of its oxygen, combine in this way, the silicate tetrahedron accounts for nearly 75 weight percent of the Earth's crust. But the silicate tetrahedron has a minus 4 charge; it is a complex anion. Its charge must be satisfied by sharing oxygens and the bonding of additional cations to the silicate tetrahedron. Those cations make up the difference between 75 and 95 percent.

4. No mineral exists with the composition SiO_3 because any compound with that composition would have a -2 charge, and all minerals are electrostatically neutral. In addition, the stereochemistry of silicon in a strong ligand field demands that it be surrounded by 4 anions.

5. The difference in hardnesses of the two would be diagnostic. Other important differences include crystal habit and differences in the indices of refraction.

6. The compositions of the Moon, Mars, and Venus are similar to that of Earth, and the laws of physics and chemistry are identical everywhere. Therefore, the minerals should be identical, although due to different chemical environments and histories, the abundances of minerals are different.

Selected Reading

A useful, short text on minerals is:
Cornelius S. Hurlbut and W. Edwin Sharp, *Dana's Minerals and How to Study Them*, 4th ed. New York: John Wiley & Sons, 1998, 235 pages.

A recent addition to mineral reference texts is:
Richard V. Gaines, H. Catherine, W. Skinner, Eugene E. Ford, Brian Moore, and Abraham Rosenzweig, *Dana's New Mineralogy: the System of Mineralogy of James Dwight Dana and Edward Salisbury Dana*. New York: John Wiley and Sons, 1997, 1872 pages.

A text that may be useful for laboratory study is:
Joseph C. Cepeda, *Introduction to Minerals and Rocks*. New York: Macmillan Publishing, 1994, 217 pp.

Cornelius Klein and Cornelius S. Hurlbut, *Manual of Mineralogy*, 21st ed. New York:John Wiley & Sons, Inc., 1993, 681 pages, is an excellent, upper-level, mineralogy text.

Another fine mineralogy text is: W. A. Deer, R. A. Howie, and J. Zussman, *An Introduction to the Rock Forming Minerals*, 2nd edition. New York, Wiley, 1992, 691 pages.

Four books that describe minerals and rocks at the introductory level are:

Joel Arem, *Rocks and Minerals*. Phoenix: Geoscience Press, 1991, 159 pages.

George W. Robinson, *Minerals: An Illustrated Exploration of the Dynamic World of Minerals and Their Properties*. New York: Simon and Schuster, 1994, describes many common and interesting minerals.

Chris Pellant, *Rocks and Minerals*. Boston: Dorling Kindersley, 1992, 256 pages.

Anna S. Sofianides and George E. Harlow, *Gems and Crystals from the American Museum of Natural History*. New York: Simon and Schuster, 1990, 208 pages.

Attractive microscopic views of both rocks and minerals are found in: W. S. MacKenzie and A. E. Adams, *A Color Atlas of Rocks and Minerals in Thin Section*. New York: John Wiley & Sons, 1994, 192 pages.

Chapter 2 Test

Multiple Choice:

1. Which of the following best describes a mineral? (a) a fundamental form of matter that cannot be broken into simpler substances by ordinary chemical processes; (b) a fundamental form of matter that can be broken into simpler substances by ordinary chemical processes; (c) a naturally occurring, inorganic solid with a characteristic chemical composition and a crystalline structure; (d) a small, dense, positively charged subatomic particle.

2. Which of the following best describes an element?
(a) a fundamental form of matter that cannot be broken into simpler substances by ordinary chemical processes; (b) a fundamental form of matter that can be broken into simpler substances by ordinary chemical processes; (c) a naturally occurring, inorganic solid with a characteristic chemical composition and a crystalline structure; (d) a small, dense, positively charged subatomic particle.

3. How many chemical elements occur naturally in the Earth's crust?
(a) 8 (b) 10 (c) 27 (d) 88 (e) 108

4. The nucleus of an atom contains
(a) electrons; (b) ions; (c) shells; (d) neutrons and protons; (e) elements

5. In a neutral atom the number of protons
(a) is greater than the number of electrons; (b) is less than the number of electrons; (c) is twice the number of electrons; (d) equals the number of electrons

6. Which has mass but no charge?
(a) proton (b) electron (c) ion (d) neutron (e) anion

7. An ion has
(a) an equal number of positive and negative charges ; (b) a net positive or negative charge; (c) mass but no charge; (d) an equal number of protons and electrons.

8. Which of the following describes a crystal?
(a) any pure substance (b) a substance composed of a single element whose atoms are arranged in a regular, ordered pattern (c) a substance whose atoms are arranged in a regular, orderly, periodically repeated pattern (d) any solid containing randomly oriented sodium and chlorine ions.

9. The shape of a crystal depends on (a) the arrangement of atoms in the crystal; (b) the chemical composition of the crystal; (c) the cleavage of the crystal; (d) the hardness and luster of the crystal.

10. Which physical properties distinguish a particular mineral from all others?
(a) streak and luster (b) fracture and faceting (c) van der Waals bonds (d) chemical composition and crystal structure

11. Calcite is a/an
(a) silicate mineral; (b) carbonate mineral; (c) clay mineral; (d) oxide mineral

12. Mohs' hardness scale
(a) is an index of the resistance of a mineral to fracture; (b) is an index of the resistance of a mineral to shattering; (c) is an index of a mineral's flexibility; (d) is an index of the resistance of a mineral to scratching.

13. Which of the following is not a rock-forming mineral?
(a) feldspar (b) galena (c) quartz (d) pyroxene

14. Which of the following is an ore mineral?
(a) feldspar (b) galena (c) quartz (d) olivine

15. A mineral that is valued for its beauty rather than for industrial use is
(a) a gem; (b) an accessory mineral; (c) an ore mineral; (d) a rock-forming mineral.

16. Geologists classify minerals
(a) according to their cations; (b) according to their protons; (c) according to their anions; (d) according to their neutrons.

17. The silicate tetrahedron consists of
(a) one central silicon ion surrounded by four oxygen ions; (b) one central oxygen ion surrounded by four silicon ions; (c) one central oxygen ion surrounded by three silicon ions; (d) one central

13

silicon ion surrounded by three oxygen ions.

18. Dolomite is a
(a) sulfide mineral; (b) phosphate mineral; (c) carbonate mineral; (d) silicate mineral.

19. Feldspar structures are based on which of the following arrangements of silicate tetrahedra?
(a) independent tetrahedra that share no oxygens; (b) framework structures in which each tetrahedron shares all four of its oxygens with adjacent tetrahedra; (c) rings of alternating silicon and oxygen atoms; (d) chains of tetrahedra in which each tetrahedron shares two oxygens with adjacent tetrahedra.

20. Which mineral group makes up more than 50 percent of the Earth's crust?
(a) mica (b) feldspar (c) quartz (d) pyroxene (e) amphibole

True or False:

1. It is not necessary for a substance to be a solid to be a mineral.

2. An element can be broken into smaller substances by ordinary chemical processes.

3. Only eight elements -oxygen, silicon, aluminum, iron, calcium, magnesium, potassium, and sodium- make up more than 98 percent of the Earth's crust.

4. The nucleus of an atom is made up of neutrons and electrons.

5. Atoms with a positive or negative charge are called ions.

6. A crystal is any substance in which atoms are arranged without a regular, orderly, periodically repeated pattern.

7. Fracture is the pattern in which a mineral breaks other than along planes of cleavage.

8. Quartz is the only common silicate mineral that contains no cations other than silicon.

9. Individual clay crystals are large enough to be seen with the naked eye.

10. In a double chain silicate, each tetrahedron shares oxygens with three other tetrahedra in the

same plane.

Completion:

1. A/an _____ is a naturally occurring, inorganic solid with a characteristic chemical composition and a crystalline structure.

2. Electrical forces that hold atoms together in compounds are _____ _____.

3. A/an _____ _____ is a planar surface that develops if a crystal grows freely without obstructions.

4. The tendency of some minerals to break along flat surfaces is _____.

5. A scale that compares the resistance of the surfaces of minerals to scratching is _____ _____ _____.

6. _____ is the color of a fine powder of a mineral.

7. _____ _____ is the weight of a substance relative to that of an equal volume of water.

8. Two ore minerals that are commonly comprised of pure metals are native _____ and _____.

9. Two common carbonate minerals are _____ and _____.

10. Every silicon atom surrounds itself with _____ oxygens in a silica tetrahedron.

11. In _____ _____ silicates adjacent tetrahedra do not share oxygens.

12. In the _____ _____, each tetrahedron links to three others in the same plane.

13. Mica and the clay minerals are _____ silicates.

14. Feldspars and quartz are _____ silicates.

Answers for Chapter 2

Multiple Choice: 1. c; 2. a; 3. d; 4. d; 5. d; 6. d; 7. b; 8. c; 9. a; 10. d; 11. b; 12. d; 13. b; 14. b; 15. a; 16. c; 17. a; 18. c; 19. b; 20. b

True or False: 1. F; 2. F; 3. T; 4. F; 5. T; 6. F; 7. T; 8. T; 9. F; 10. F

Completion: 1. mineral; 2. chemical bonds; 3. crystal face 4. cleavage; 5. Moh's hardness scale; 6. streak; 7. Specific gravity; 8. gold, silver; 9. calcite and dolomite; 10. four; 11. independent tetrahedra; 12. sheet silicates; 13. sheet; 14. framework.

CHAPTER 3

Rocks

Discussion

We begin this chapter by explaining that an understanding of rocks and how they form provides a foundation to understanding much about the geologic history of the Earth's crust. The chapter then describes the rock cycle as a paradigm of the processes by which, over geologic time, rocks constantly change from one to another of the three main categories of rocks: igneous, sedimentary, and metamorphic. We stress the nature of Earth systems interactions among the atmosphere, hydrosphere, biosphere, and geosphere in the rock cycle.

The rest of the chapter explains the processes by which igneous, sedimentary, and metamorphic rocks form, describes how common rocks of each type are classified and named, and discusses the most common kinds of rocks in the Earth's crust.

In an introductory Earth Science text, the subject of rocks is one that can cover several chapters, and go on at great length because of the nearly infinite variety of rock types and processes by which they form. We have chosen to cover igneous, sedimentary, and metamorphic rocks in a single chapter by taking advantage of the fact that only a few kinds of rocks are common and encountered frequently by most of us, students and professionals alike. Those few, abundant rock types deserve to be stressed, and the myriad others can be ignored in an introductory course. Among the igneous rocks, we describe granite and basalt, rhyolite, gabbro, andesite, diorite, and peridotite (because it is the material of the mantle). We focus on shale, sandstone, and limestone among the sedimentary rocks, and slate, schist, gneiss, and marble as metamorphic rocks. We concentrate on the few, common rock types because we feel that it is more meaningful to an introductory student to learn to recognize common rocks, and understand the processes that form them, than to be impressed (or depressed) by the great number of uncommon rocks that have been named.

We continue to emphasize the interactions among rocks, atmosphere, water, and organisms where appropriate throughout this chapter. A Focus On Box describes the origins and effects of radon gas.

Answers to Discussion Questions

1. Magma begins to rise as soon as it forms because it is substantially (about 10 percent, on the average) less dense than the rocks surrounding it. The liquid, mobile magma shoulders aside the plastic solid rock and rises.

2. In the San Juans, rising granitic and intermediate magma erupted as ash flow tuffs and related volcanic rocks. As the magma rose, portions solidified at shallow depth in the crust. Thus, both intrusive and extrusive rocks formed from the same magma, or from closely related magmas.

3. Texture is the simplest clue to volcanic or plutonic origin of a rock. If an igneous rock is uniformly medium or coarse grained, it is probably plutonic. If it is glassy or very fine grained, it is probably volcanic. However, texture is not always reliable as an indicator of volcanic or plutonic origin. A thin dike or sill (plutonic) may have a fine texture if it was intruded into cool country rock. Some granitic volcanics are medium, or even coarse, grained, particularly if they crystallized at depth to a considerable extent before rising and flowing onto the surface. Thus, it is not always possible to distinguish volcanic or plutonic origin from a hand sample of a rock. It is much better to be able to study field relationships.

4. This question should have a simple answer, but it does not, partly because of the great variety of rock types in each of the three main categories. For most rocks, the following criteria work to identify them as igneous, sedimentary, or metamorphic.
      Most igneous rocks are silicates, contain predominantly feldspar, show igneous textures (of which there is a wide variety), and contain characteristic mineral assemblages summarized in Figure 3-7 of the text. In the field, they show intrusive or extrusive relationships with country rock.
      Most sedimentary rocks show bedding or other sedimentary structures, and most clastic rocks show rounding of the grains. Feldspar is typically much less abundant in sedimentary rocks than in igneous rocks, because it weathers much more easily than quartz or clay minerals, which are the most common minerals in clastic sedimentary rocks. Many sedimentary rocks contain fossils. Limestone is predominantly calcite (or dolomite), and has an unmistakable appearance to an experienced field geologist. This latter observation frustrates rather that helps introductory students, however.
      Many metamorphic rocks show metamorphic foliation, but it is sometimes difficult to explain to an introductory student how to distinguish metamorphic layering from sedimentary layering. But metamorphic rocks usually also show interlocking grain boundaries rather than the rounded grains characteristic of clastic sedimentary rocks. Most metamorphic rocks contain minerals characteristic of metamorphism, such as chlorite, micas, garnet, and a variety of amphiboles. However, many of those minerals are not really unique to metamorphic rocks.
      An additional difficulty in distinguishing among the three rock categories arises with rocks that fall on a boundary between two categories. An example of this type of rock is an air-fall tuff. It is both igneous and sedimentary. Similarly, a basal surge deposit of an ash flow tuff from a violent caldera eruption may show beautiful cross bedding. Another example of a boundary

transcendent rock is the metamorphosed granite that comprises most continental basement rock.

This question is an excellent one to get students thinking about identifying rocks, and about how they form.

5. Sediment originates by weathering. Feldspar is the most abundant mineral in the Earth's crust. Feldspar (and other aluminosilicates) predominantly form clay minerals when they weather. Therefore, clays are the most abundant products of weathering of the Earth's crust. When clays are deposited and lithified, they form shale. Since clay is the most abundant weathering product, shale is the most common sedimentary rock.

6. Sedimentary clasts become rounded during transport by water or wind. The rounding occurs as the clasts bounce against one another, or against bedrock during transport. Well-rounded grains imply a relatively long time and distance of transport, whereas angular grains imply less time and distance. Large clasts such as cobbles and boulders, however, commonly become well-rounded within short times and distances from their source. Sand and silt become rounded more slowly.

Angular clasts may also imply that water or wind was not the transport medium. They are common in debris flows and glacial deposits, where the viscosity of the medium cushions the grain impacts and slows rounding.

7. Sedimentary structures such as mud cracks and raindrop imprints indicate shallow water deposition. The water must have been shallow enough that occasionally the original mud was exposed at the surface so that raindrops created the imprints by falling on a surface unprotected by a layer of water. Similarly, most mudcracks form in a subaerial environment, where wet mud dries and shrinks. It might be appropriate here to mention submarine syneresis cracking as an example of the principle that not everything that looks, waddles, and quacks like a duck, IS a duck.

8. Contact metamorphic rocks commonly form a relatively small halo around the intrusion that caused the metamorphism, with metamorphic grade increasing toward the contact. Regional metamorphic rocks normally occur over a much larger area, and the metamorphic grade may bear little or no relation to plutons. Contact metamorphic rocks normally show no foliation, whereas most regionally metamorphic rocks are foliated.

9. The original sedimentary layering may be preserved as compositional layering in the metamorphic rock. Thus a metamorphosed sandstone layer will have a different composition from that of an adjacent metamorphosed shale layer. However, bedding within a single sedimentary rock type is often completely lost as slaty cleavage, schistosity, or gneissic textures

develop.

10. If country rock similar to granite in composition (this includes most of the continental crust) is heated to the highest grades of metamorphism, the rock may partially melt to form granitic magma. That magma may remain in small veins in the country rock to form migmatite, or it may coalesce and rise through the crust to form a granitic pluton.

11. We emphasize the importance of Earth systems interactions among the geosphere, the atmosphere, the hydrosphere, and the biosphere in rock cycle processes throughout this chapter, and discuss it specifically in Section 3.1. This question is designed to point out the importance of all Earth systems to all aspects of Earth science, even those as traditionally bedrock geology-oriented as the origins of rocks.

Selected Reading

Several texts that cover a wide variety of rocks and rock types are:

R. Dietrich and B. Skinner, *Rocks and Rock Minerals*. New York: John Wiley & Sons, 1979.

P. Hess, *Origins of Igneous Rocks*. Boston: Harvard University Press, 1989.

Donald Hyndman, *Petrology of Igneous and Metamorphic Rocks,* 2nd ed. New York: McGraw-Hill, 1985.

K. Krauskopf, *Introduction to Geochemistry*, 2nd ed. New York: McGraw-Hill, 1979.

Loren A. Raymond, *Petrology - The Study of Igneous, Sedimentary, and Metamorphic Rocks*. Chicago: Wm. C. Brown Publishers, 1995.

Sedimentary rocks are spectacularly visible across much of the American Southwest. A guide to the Colorado Plateau is given in Halka Chronic, *Pages of Stone: Geology of Western National Parks and Monuments, Vol. 4, Grand Canyon and the Plateau Country*. Seattle: The Mountaineers, 1988.

Metamorphic rocks
        Several texts and reference books describe metamorphism and metamorphic rocks:
E.G. Ehlers and H. Blatt, *Petrology: Igneous, Sedimentary, and Metamorphic*. W.H. Freeman &

Co, 1995.

A. Miyashiro, *Metamorphic Petrology*. New York: Oxford University Press, Inc., 1994.

L.L. Perchuk, editor, *Progress in Metamorphic & Magmatic Petrology: A Memorial Volume in Honor of D.S. Korzhinskiy*. New York: Cambridge University Press, 1991.

B.W. Yardley, W.S. MacKenzie, and C. Guilford, *Atlas of Metamorphic Rocks & Their Textures*. New York: Halstead Press, 1990.

Chapter 3 Test

Multiple Choice:

1. The rock cycle describes geologic processes in which
(a) rocks remain unchanged over time; (b) igneous and metamorphic rocks do not change over time, but sedimentary rocks do; (c) all types of rocks change from one type to another over time; (d) sedimentary rocks form directly from molten magma.

2. Igneous rocks form by
(a) lithification of sediment; (b) solid state textural or mineralogical alteration of existing rocks; (c) solidification of magma; (d) precipitation of seawater.

3. When a silicate rock melts, the resulting magma _____ by about _____.
(a) expands, 1 percent (b) expands, 10 percent; (c) contracts, 1 percent (d) contracts, 10 percent.

4. Intrusive igneous rocks form when magma solidifies
(a) on the Earth's surface; (b) within the Earth; (c) on the sea floor.

5. Extrusive igneous rocks form when
(a) magma solidifies within the Earth; (b) magma solidifies within the asthenosphere; (c) sediment cements together; (d) magma erupts and solidifies on the Earth's surface.

6. The most abundant igneous rock in continental crust is
(a) basalt; (b) granite; (c) rhyolite; (d) porphyry: (e) gabbro.

7. _____ has the same mineral content as granite?
(a) Basalt (b) Diorite (c) Rhyolite (d) Andesite (e) Gabbro

8. Obsidian
(a) forms deep in the crust; (b) is finely crystalline; (c) is volcanic glass; (d) is a metamorphic rock; (e) forms from weathering of granite.

9. Which of these pairs of igneous rocks is mismatched?
(a) granite-rhyolite (b) diorite-andesite (c) gabbro-basalt (d) diorite-peridotite

10. Which igneous rock is rare in the crust but abundant in the mantle?

22

(a) peridotite (b) obsidian (c) basalt (d) gabbro (e) diorite

11. Which of these igneous rocks is the most abundant rock type in oceanic crust?
(a) rhyolite (b) basalt (c) peridotite (d) granite

12. Rocks formed at or near the Earth's surface from the accumulated products of weathering and erosion are
(a) metamorphic rocks; (b) igneous rocks; (c) magma; (d) sedimentary rocks.

13. Sedimentary rock makes up
(a) about 5 percent of the Earth's mantle; (b) about 0.5 percent of the Earth's crust; (c) about 5 percent of the Earth's crust; (d) about 50 percent of the Earth's crust.

14. Sedimentary rocks cover about ____ percent of the Earth's continents.
(a) 5; (b) 25; (c) 75; (d) 95.

15. Clastic sediment consists of
(a) fragments of weathered rock or shells; (b) dissolved ions; (c) precipitated minerals; (d) solidified magma.

16. Coal is a
(a) clastic sedimentary rock; (b) organic sedimentary rock; (c) chemical sedimentary rock; (d) igneous rock; (e) metamorphic rock.

17. The process of _____ convert loose sediment to solid rock.
(a) partial melting; (b) sedimentation; (c) lithification; (d) metamorphism.

18. Lithified sand is
(a) conglomerate; (b) granite; (c) sandstone; (d) shale.

19. Lithified clay is
(a) conglomerate; (b) granite; (c) sandstone; (d) shale.

20. Which of these minerals commonly forms by evaporation of sea water?
(a) halite; (b) clay; (c) feldspar; (d) quartz.

21. Limestone is composed mainly of
(a) halite; (b) clay; (c) calcite; (d) precipitated quartz; (e) lithified quartz sand.

22. Sedimentary bedding forms as
(a) sediment is deposited; (b) sedimentary rocks are eroded; (c) sedimentary rocks become metamorphosed; (d) tectonic forces deform sedimentary rocks.

23. Graded bedding
(a) forms in dry windy environments; (b) forms when sediment is deposited from a submarine landslide; (c) forms in sediment deposited by a glacier; (d) forms in sediment carried by a debris flow.

24. Metamorphic rock forms when
(a) magma cools and solidifies; (b) igneous, sedimentary, or other metamorphic rocks change because of high temperature and/or pressure, or compositional changes, or are deformed during mountain building; (c) seawater precipitates; (d) sediments are lithified.

25. When limestone metamorphoses to marble,
(a) the texture changes, but the mineral composition does not; (b) the texture and mineral composition change, but there is no deformation; (c) the texture and mineral composition change, and the rock is deformed; (d) the only change is that the rock becomes foliated.

26. Slaty cleavage is a set of parallel fractures found in many metamorphic rocks that
(a) forms perpendicular to the direction of tectonic stress and commonly cuts across original sedimentary bedding; (b) forms commonly during burial metamorphism; (c) forms commonly during contact metamorphism; (d) forms parallel to the direction of tectonic stress and commonly lies parallel to original sedimentary bedding.

27. An example of a metamorphic change in which the new rock has different minerals and a new texture is the transformation of
(a) limestone to marble; (b) quartz sandstone to quartzite; (c) shale to schist; (d) all of the above.

28. Burial metamorphism
(a) occurs when hot magma rises near the surface; (b) occurs during mountain building; (c) forms slaty cleavage; (d) produces unfoliated metamorphic rocks.

29. The most widespread metamorphic rocks exposed at the Earth's surface are formed by
(a) regional metamorphism; (b) hydrothermal metamorphism; (c) contact metamorphism; (d) burial metamorphism.

30. Contact metamorphism refers to metamorphism
(a) that affects broad regions of the crust; (b) caused by intrusion of cold magma into hot rocks;
(c) caused by the intrusion of hot magma into cooler rocks; (d) that is usually accompanied by
deformation.

True or False:

1. The crust contains a greater concentration of silica than the mantle.

2. The most important mechanism for magma formation at a spreading center is pressure release.

3. The most important mechanism for magma formation in a subduction zone is probably
pressure release.

4. The temperature of magma varies from about 600°C to 1400°C.

5. Volcanic rocks are usually medium- or coarse-grained, whereas plutonic rocks are fine-grained.

6. Gabbro is mineralogically identical to basalt.

7. Obsidian is volcanic glass made up of coarse crystals.

8. Basalt melts at a higher temperature than granite.

9. Continental crust is typically thicker than oceanic crust.

10. When a silicate rock melts, the magma that forms is 10 percent more dense than the rock.

11. Granite is the most abundant igneous rock on the sea floor.

12. The most common sedimentary rocks are shale, sandstone, and limestone.

13. In certain environments dissolved ions may precipitate directly to form sandstone.

14. Calcite, quartz, and iron oxides are the most common cements in sedimentary rocks.

15. Evaporites form when evaporation of water concentrates dissolved ions to the point where

they precipitate from solution.

16. Fluids aid metamorphic reactions by making ions and molecules mobile.

17. The upper temperature limit of metamorphism is the point at which rocks melt.

18. Marble is made of calcite.

19. Foliation is metamorphic layering.

20. Contact metamorphic rocks are usually foliated.

21. Burial metamorphism is occurring today deep within the Mississippi delta.

22. Regional metamorphism is usually accompanied by deformation, so the rocks are foliated.

23. Most hydrothermal alteration is caused by circulating ground water.

Completion:

1. Geologists separate rocks into three classes based on how they form: _____, _____, and _____ rocks.

2. Igneous rocks that erupt and solidify at the Earth's surface are _____.

3. If magma and crystals suddenly erupt to the Earth's surface a fine-grained rock with large crystals called _____ forms.

4. The size, shape and arrangement of igneous mineral grains in a rock define its _____.

5. Igneous rocks with abundant magnesium and iron are _____.

6. Igneous rocks that have a composition between mafic and felsic are termed _____.

7. The igneous rock that is the most abundant in the mantle is _____.

8. The fine-grained volcanic equivalent of granite is _____.

9. All solid particles eroded from weathered rock and transported and deposited by water, wind, glaciers, and gravity are referred to as _____ _____.

10. Thin bedding along which shale easily splits is called _____.

11. As peat is buried and compacted by overlying sediment, it converts to _____.

12. Calcite-rich carbonate rocks are called _____.

13. Chemical reactions that occur in solids without melting are _____ _____ reactions.

14. The process by which rocks and minerals change in response to changing temperature, pressure, and/or composition within the crust is _____.

15. Limestone metamorphoses to _____ as calcite crystals grow in size.

16. Parallel growth of mica and chlorite during metamorphism and deformation of shales produces _____ _____.

17. The maximum temperature and pressure a rock undergoes determines its metamorphic - _____.

18. Direct heating causes _____ metamorphism near the edge of a pluton.

19. Hot water causes _____ metamorphism.

20. The _____ _____ of a rock is the intensity of metamorphism that formed the rock.

Answers for Chapter 3

Multiple Choice: 1. c; 2. c; 3. b; 4. b; 5. d; 6. b; 7. c; 8. c; 9. d; 10. a; 11. b; 12. d; 13. c; 14. c; 15. a; 16. b; 17. c; 18. c; 19. d; 20. a; 21. c; 22. a; 23. b; 24. b; 25. a; 26. a; 27. c; 28. d; 29. a; 30. c.

True/False: 1. T; 2. T; 3. F; 4. T; 5. F; 6. T; 7. F; 8. T; 9. T; 10. F; 11. F; 12. T; 13. F; 14. T; 15. T; 16. T; 17. T; 18. T; 19. T; 20. F; 21. T; 22. T; 23. T.

Completion: 1. igneous, sedimentary, and metamorphic; 2. volcanic or extrusive; 3. porphyry; 4. texture; 5. mafic; 6. intermediate rocks; 7. peridotite; 8. rhyolite; 9. clastic sediment; 10. fissility; 11. coal; 12. limestone; 13. solid state; 14. metamorphism; 15. marble; 16. slaty cleavage; 17. grade; 18. contact; 19. hydrothermal; 20. metamorphic grade.

CHAPTER 4

Geologic Time: A Story in the Rocks

Discussion:

Geology is largely a science of events that have occurred in the past. When did that continent assemble, that mountain range rise, or sediment accumulate in a basin? In Chapter 1, we introduced the great length of geologic time and two important consequences of that magnitude: Slow, almost imperceptible events and rare, catastrophic events both become significant over the long expanse of Earth history.

We open this chapter by distinguishing between relative and absolute age. We then discuss basic principles for relative age determination, both in the rocks and in fossils imbedded within the rocks. This discussion is followed by a brief explanation of the processes and tools of geologic correlation.

The section on relative time is followed by a discussion of absolute time. In the subsection "What is Measured by a Radiometric Age Date" students are encouraged to understand that age determination involves much more than sending a rock to a laboratory; data are only meaningful if interpreted correctly. The Focus On box, "Carbon-14 dating," outlines an important dating technique with a mechanism that is different from other parent/daughter pairs.

We end the chapter with a brief outline of the Geologic Time Scale and the events that occurred during the major subdivisions in Earth history.

Answers to Discussion Questions

1. Many of the examples given in this Chapter were oriented toward interpretation of sedimentary rocks, but Earth-like sedimentary processes do not occur on the Moon. However, similar thought processes can be used. If a basalt flow fills the bottom of an impact crater, we can deduce that the eruption occurred after the meteorite impact; if a small crater lies within a larger one, we can deduce that the small impact occurred after the larger one. Lunar and planetary geologists also use crater abundances to determine the order of geological events. If one region contains a much lower crater abundance than a nearby region, we can assume that tectonic or erosional events obliterated old craters in that region.

2. The rock is between 520 and 505 million years old.

3. Abundant, well-preserved fossils exist mainly in Phanerozoic rocks, so even with no further

information, you could say that the rock was probably no older than 543 million years old. Of course, with a knowledge of fossils and evolutionary history, you could give the age more precisely. Additional information is available by comparing your sample with rocks above and below it as discussed in the principles outlined in the text.

4. Assuming that the radiometric date on the biotite is unaffected by weathering, (a) would give the cooling age of the granite; (b) would give the time that the schist cooled through the argon retention temperature of the biotite (assuming that metamorphic temperature initially rose above that temperature); (c) would give the age of the igneous or metamorphic event during which the biotite formed, not the age of deposition of the sand. The biotite must be detrital, since it rarely or never forms in sedimentary environments. In all three cases it is necessary to compensate for initial argon uptake during formation of the biotite. In general, this question can be used to get into as detailed a discussion of the complexities of radiometric dating as the professor wishes.

5. The K/Ar age would be lower than the actual age of the granite. Loss of daughter isotope gives the false impression that the daughter has been accumulating for less time than the real age of the rock.

6. Because you can date a rock from fossil assemblages, a study of fossils would tell you if the deeply buried rocks are younger than those above them. Of course radiometric dating would also provide the same answer. Other clues would help you determine whether or not the rocks were overturned. For example, raindrop imprints, mudcracks, ripple marks, glacial striations, and many other features in rock occur on the top surface. If these features are facing downward, then you can infer that the rock was overturned.

7. Obviously you can't walk from Ohio to Wyoming for a visual correlation, and even if you did chose to walk, the outcrop wouldn't be exposed for the entire distance. Thus you would correlate the rocks using the techniques discussed in the chapter, such as index fossils and key beds.

8. Many such analogies can be constructed. Some can be based on familiar units of measure, such as a mile, a kilometer, a day, a year, etc. Others can be local examples, such as the distance to the next town, from a fraternity house to the nearest sorority, and so forth.

9. Ecosystems change with climate, so fossil assemblages would reflect temperature and rainfall. Other indicators such as rain drop imprints, mud cracks, ripple marks, deep cuts from stream erosion or flood deposition zones indicate wet environments. Alluvial fans, pediments, and bajadas are abundant in regions with intermittent rainfall. Sand dunes occur on coastlines or in

dry environments. Glacial striations form in cold wet climates.

Selected Reading

Many books and articles document the evolution and history of life. A few that we find useful include:

Anna K. Behrensmeyer et al., *Terrestrial Ecosystems Through Time*. Chicago: University of Chicago Press, 1993, 588 pages.

Stefan Bengston, *Early Life on Earth*. New York: Columbia University Press, 1994, 372 pages.

Peter Bowler, *Life's Splendid Drama: Evolutionary Biology and the Reconstruction of Life's Ancestry, 1860-1949*. Chicago: University of Chicago Press, 1996, 525 pages.

Peter Doyle, Matthew R. Bennett, and Alistair N. Baxter, *The Key to Earth History: An Introduction to Stratigraphy*. New York: John Wiley, 1994, 231 pages.

Christian de Duve, *Vital Dust, The Origin and Evolution of Life on Earth*. New York: Basic Books, 1995, 362 pages.

Frederick Hadleigh, ed. *American Beginnings: The Prehistory and Paleoecology of Beringia*. Chicago: University of Chicago Press, 1996, 576 pages.

J.D. MacDougall, *A Short History of Planet Earth*. New York: John Wiley Publishing, 1996, 266 pages.

Roger Osborne and Donald Tarling, eds. *The Historical Atlas of the Earth: A Visual Celebration of Earth's Physical Past*. New York: H. Holt, 1996, 192 pages.

For more information about fossils and extinctions we recommend:

Walter Alvarez, *T.rex and the Crater of Doom*. Princeton, NJ: Princeton University Press, 1997, 185 pages.

Kenneth Carpenter, Karl F. Hirsch, and John R. Horner, eds., *Dinosaur Eggs and Babies*. New York: Cambridge University Press, 1994, 388 pages.

W. G. Chaloner and A. Hallam eds., *Evolution and Extinction*. New York: Cambridge University

Press, 1994, 264 pages.

Niles Eldredge, *Fossils: The Evolution and Extinction of Species*. Princeton, NJ: Princeton University Press, 1997.

David E. Fastovsky and David B. Weischampel, *The Evolution and Extinctions of the Dinosaurs*. New York: Cambridge University Press, 1996, 476 pages.

Richard Fortey, *Fossils: The Key to the Past*. Boston: Harvard University Press, 1994, 187 pages.

Stephen J. Gould, ed., *The Book of Life: An Illustrated History of the Evolution of Life on Earth*. New York: W. W. Norton, 1993, 256 pages.

Richardo Levi-Setti, *Trilobites*. Chicago: University of Chicago Press, 1993, 342 pages.

Charles Officer and Jake Page, *The Great Dinosaur Extinction Controversy*. New York: Addison-Wesley, 1996, 209 pages.

Ian Tattersall, *The Fossil Trail: How we Know What We Think We Know about Human Evolution*. Oxford: Oxford University Press, 1995, 276 pages.

We also recommend one of our own texts: G. Thompson, J. Turk, and H Levin, *Earth Past and Present*. Philadelphia: Saunders College Publishing, 1995, 664 pages.

Chapter 4 Test

Multiple Choice:

1. The principle of crosscutting relationships states that
(a) sediment usually accumulates in horizontal layers; (b) sedimentary rocks generally become younger from bottom to top; (c) sedimentary rocks must be older than an intruding dike; (d) rocks can be dated by studying radioactive decay of the elements.

2. An unconformity in which tectonic activity tilted older sedimentary rock layers before younger sediment has accumulated is
(a) a nonconformity; (b) an angular unconformity; (c) a disconformity; (d) conformable.

3. In a disconformity
(a) the sedimentary layers above and below the unconformity are parallel; (b) the sedimentary layers below the unconformity are tilted; (c) sedimentary rocks lie on older metamorphic rocks; (d) sedimentary rocks lie on older igneous rocks.

4. Imagine that you found two sandstone beds about 200 kilometers apart. The rock in one region was similar to the rock in the other, but one bed was several million years older than the other. From this information, you would conclude that
(a) the two beds were time correlated; (b) both beds would contain the same index fossils; (c) the two beds were lithologically correlated; (d) a and b; (e) b and c.

5. To be useful, an index fossil is produced by an organism that
(a) evolved early in the history of the Earth; (b) was rare on the Earth's surface; (c) existed for a relatively short time; (d) lived in a unique and rare environment.

6. To measure absolute age, a geologist uses
(a) the principle of original horizontality; (b) the principle of cross-cutting relationships; (c) the principle of superposition; (d) radiometric dating.

7. Different isotopes are atoms of the same element with different numbers of _____.
(a) neutrons (b) protons (c) electrons

8. The half-life of potassium-40 is 1.3 billion years. If a rock that formed at the beginning of the Proterozoic Eon originally contained 5 grams of potassium-40, about how much potassium-40

would be left in that rock today?
(a) 0.0125 grams; (b) 0.125 grams; (c) 1.25 grams; (d) 0.25 grams; (e) 2.5 grams.

9. In radiometric dating, scientists measure
(a) the number of protons in a sample; (b) the number of neutrons in a sample; (c) the ratio of protons to neutrons; (d) the ratio of daughter isotopes to parent isotopes.

10. The largest unit of geologic time is a/an
(a) era; (b) epoch; (c) eon; (d) period.

11. There have been no fossils found from the
(a) Proterozoic Eon; (b) Phanerozoic Eon; (c) Hadean Eon; (d) Archean Eon.

12. Precambrian refers to all the time before the start of the
(a) Proterozoic Eon; (b) Phanerozoic Eon; (c) Hadean Eon; (d) Archean Eon.

13. The dinosaurs thrived during the
(a) Paleozoic era; (b) Mesozoic era; (c) Cenozoic era; (d) Proterozoic Eon.

14. Fish, amphibians, and reptiles all evolved during the
(a) Paleozoic era; (b) Mesozoic era; (c) Cenozoic era; (d) Proterozoic Eon.

15. Humans evolved during the
(a) Paleozoic era; (b) Mesozoic era; (c) Cenozoic era; (d) Proterozoic Eon.

True or False:

1. Relative age dating is based on the principal that in order for an event to affect a rock, the rock must exist first.

2. Younger layers of sediment always accumulate below older layers.

3. In an angular unconformity, older sedimentary beds were tilted and eroded before younger layers were deposited.

4. The principle of superposition assures us that sedimentary rocks formed continuously from 2 billion to 200 million years ago.

5. The principle of faunal succession states that fossil organisms succeeded one another through time in a definite and recognizable order and that the relative ages of rocks can therefore be recognized from their fossils.

6. The shorter the time span that a species existed, the more precisely an index fossil can be used to determine the age of a rock.

7. Potassium-40 decomposes naturally to form either of two other isotopes, argon-40 or calcium-40.

8. When a parent isotope decomposes, the quantity of daughter isotopes in a sample increases with time.

9. Sedimentary rocks from the Phanerozoic Eon contain only microscopic fossils of single-celled organisms.

10. The Paleozoic era ended abruptly about 245 million years ago when a catastrophic mass extinction wiped out a great number of species both on land and in the oceans.

Completion:

1. _____ _____ lists the order in which geologic events occurred.

2. _____ _____ measures time in years.

3. The principle of _____ _____ is based on the observation that sediment usually accumulates in horizontal layers.

4. The principle of _____ states that sedimentary rocks usually become younger from bottom to top.

5. A basalt dike cutting older sedimentary rocks is an example of the principle of _____ _____ _____.

6. A/an _____ is an unconformity in which sedimentary rocks lie on igneous or metamorphic rocks.

7. Use of fossils to determine the relative age of a rock employs the principle of _____ _____.

8. Matching rocks of similar ages from different localities is _____.

9. A/an _____ _____ is a thin, widespread sedimentary layer that was deposited rapidly and synchronously over a wide area and is easily recognized.

10. Mammals evolved during the _____ era.

Answers for Chapter 4

Multiple Choice 1. c; 2. b; 3. a; 4. c; 5. c; 6. d; 7. a; 8. c; 9. d; 10. c; 11. c; 12. b; 13. b; 14. a; 15. c

True or False 1. T; 2. F; 3. T; 4. F; 5. T; 6. T; 7. T; 8. T; 9. F; 10. T

Completion 1. Relative age; 2. Absolute age; 3. original horizontality; 4. superposition; 5. cross cutting relationships; 6. nonconformity; 7. faunal succession; 8. correlation; 9. key bed; 10. Mesozoic

CHAPTER 5

The Active Earth: Plate Tectonics

Discussion

The plate tectonics theory is the modern foundation for explaining the Earth's internal processes and their consequences. It provides an integrative framework for descriptions of igneous processes, metamorphism, earthquakes, volcanic eruptions, origins of geologic structures, and evolution of continents and ocean basins. The theory has also become integral to discussions of Earth systems interactions and surface processes. Volcanic events affect climate and the composition of the atmosphere, and thus affect weathering, erosion, and sedimentary processes. Rates of plate movement affect sea level, affecting coastal processes and causing marine flooding of continents and deposition of platform sedimentary rocks at times of high sea level. Tectonic uplift changes stream profiles and alters alluvial erosion and deposition. Some of the Earth's ice ages are related to clustering of continents about the polar regions.

Because the plate tectonics theory has become so broadly integrated into geologic thinking and the teaching of geology at the introductory level, we have written a simple, straightforward introduction to the most important aspects of the theory as Chapter 5 in the second edition of Earth Science and the Environment. This chapter provides a background for the following chapters which can then be read in virtually any order chosen by a professor. Additional aspects of the theory are integrated into subsequent chapters, so that a student expands upon the introductory material in Chapter 5 as he or she reads and learns about subsequent topics.

Chapter 5 begins with a very brief overview of the plate tectonics model, describing the lithosphere, asthenosphere, and tectonic plates, and stressing the point that most tectonic activity occurs at plate boundaries. We then describe the Earth's layers in more detail, emphasizing the importance of the lithosphere and asthenosphere to the plate tectonic theory. Section 5.2 describes divergent, convergent, and transform plate boundaries in oceanic and continental crust, and discusses features of plate boundaries such as the mid-oceanic ridge system and subduction zones.

Section 5.3 summarizes the nature of a tectonic plate, and Section 5.4 describes the interactions among plate tectonic activities, atmospheric composition, climate, oceanic processes, and plants and animals. The chapter finishes with descriptions of current hypotheses explaining the causes of plate motions and the role of deep mantle convection, the concept of supercontinent cycles, and isostasy. A Focus On box at the chapter's end describes Alfred Wegener's continental drift hypothesis as a precursor to the plate tectonics theory.

Answers to Discussion Questions

1. A unifying theory is beneficial to any science because it allows scientists to understand a wide range of apparently different phenomena, such as volcanic eruptions, earthquakes, and migrating continents, as phenomena that are causally related to each other, and to most other events. In a very real sense, it makes a science much easier to understand than would be the case in the absence of a unifying theory.

2. Some geologists think that continental glaciers melt very rapidly during a major glacial retreat. Solid Earth geophysicists estimate the rate at which the mantle can flow to accommodate isostatic adjustments, such as those that accompany melting of icecaps. Comparison of the two rates suggests that the time required for melting of the Greenland icecap may be much less than the time required for isostatic rebound to occur. Thus, the continental crust of central Greenland might remain submerged for thousands of years if the icecap were to melt relatively rapidly. In the long run, however, isostatic adjustment would cause all of Greenland to rise above sea level following melting of its icecap.

3. The answers to these questions depend on the measurements of students' own classrooms and campuses.

4. Most continental mountain chains form at convergent plate boundaries either where subduction of oceanic lithosphere occurs at a continental margin (the Andes along the west coast of South America, the Cascade and Coast Ranges of the Pacific Northwest), or where two continents collide (the Himalayas). Both environments involve the generation of huge quantities of magma. In the case of continent-continent collisions, the magma forms when an Andean margin is created before the continents themselves collide. Both environments also involve deformation of vast regions near the respective plate boundaries. As a result of deformation and the addition of magma to continental crust, immense mountain chains such as the Andes and the Himalayas rise near these plate boundaries.

Continental rifting results from development of a divergent plate boundary in continental crust. High escarpments result from normal faulting, and volcanic mountains form in such environments, as in the East African Rift. Generally, little folding or deformation other than normal faulting occur in continental rifts because the stress is mainly extensional.

A transform plate boundary exists along the San Andreas fault in western California. Here, small, folded and faulted mountain ranges are rising along the fault zone. Somewhat similar ranges are forming along the great strike-slip faults in Tibet, China, and Mongolia, north of the Himalayas. Although this region is not a transform plate boundary, the huge strike-slip faults generate similar tectonic forces and structures.

5. Astronomers look for volcanoes, high plateaus, and deep trenches, which may have formed by tectonic activity. Studies of meteorite craters are also useful. All planets in the Solar System were bombarded by swarms of meteorites during the first half-billion years. Thus, initially all planets were pock-marked by meteorite impact craters. Any later tectonic activity would produce features that would cross-cut or obliterate those craters. Features that would indicate tectonic activity include mountain ranges, rift valleys, lava flows, trenches (like oceanic trenches on Earth), and volcanic cones. It would be necessary to distinguish features formed by tectonic activity from those created by weathering and erosion, which also would cross-cut or obliterate impact craters.

6. The maximum height of a mountain is determined by the strength of rock, the force of gravity, and the isostatic buoyancy. Mars has one tenth the mass of the Earth, so its gravity is less. Because it is smaller, the interior has cooled more than that of the Earth, so its asthenosphere is more rigid. As a result, the Martian surface can support higher and more massive mountains.

7. The volume of a sphere increases in proportion to the cube of its radius ($V = 4/3$ pi r^3). Thus, although the core is thicker than the mantle, the larger radius of the mantle results in its much greater volume. Students can work the answer out quantitatively using the above equation and the dimensions of the core and mantle given in the question.

8.   Crust: 0.8 millimeters to 1.3 centimeters.
     Lithosphere: 1.2 centimeters to 2 centimeters.
     Asthenosphere: 4 centimeters.
     Mantle: 44 centimeters.
     Core: 54 centimeters.

9. The Eurasian plate is mostly continent, the Pacific plate is mostly ocean basin, and the North American, South American, and African plates are roughly equally composed of continent and ocean.

10. Interactions among plate tectonics processes and Earth systems are described and discussed at length in the Opening Essay to Unit II titled "Plate Tectonics and Earth Systems", and in the short subsection at the end of Section 5.4, titled "Effects on the Hydrosphere, Atmosphere, and Biosphere". We hope this question will lead students to read the Essay if they have not done so already.

Selected Reading

Several books that describe current plate tectonics concepts are:
Philip Kearey and F.J. Vine, *Global Tectonics, Second Edition.* Cambridge, MA: Blackwell Science, Inc, 1996, 348 pages.

Eldrige M. Moores, ed., *Shaping the Earth: Tectonics of Continents and Oceans.* New York: W. H. Freeman, 1990, 206 pages.

Walter Sullivan, *Continents in Motion: The New Earth Debate.* New York: American Institute of Physics, 1991, 430 pages.

An Yin and Mark Harrison, eds., *The Tectonic Evolution of Asia.* New York: Cambridge University Press, 1996, 678 pages.

Sea-floor plate tectonics are discussed in:
Joseph Cone, *Fire Under the Sea: Volcanic Hot Springs on the Ocean Floor.* New York: Morrow, 1991, 285 pages.

An excellent little book that gives Wegener's own version of his story is:
A. Wegener: *The Origins of Continents and Oceans.* Translated from the 4th revised German edition, 1929, by J. Biram. London: Methuen, 1966.

A well-written and informative description of the tectonic evolution of western North America is:
John McPhee, *Assembling California.* New York: Farrar Straus Giroux, 1993, 304 pages.

Chapter 5 Test

Multiple Choice:

1. Average oceanic crust is _____ kilometers thick whereas average continental crust is _____ kilometers thick.
(a) 4 to 7, 20 to 40 (b) 50 to 100, 200 to 400 (c) 20 to 40, 5 to 10 (d) 200 to 400, 50 to 100

2. Oceanic crust is composed mainly of
(a) granite; (b) iron and nickel; (c) basalt; (d) shale and limestone.

3. The outer 75 to 125 kilometers of the Earth including both the crust and upper mantle consists of
(a) molten iron and nickel of the outer core; (b) hard, strong rock of the lithosphere; (c) weak, plastic rock of the asthenosphere; (d) solid iron and nickel of the inner core.

4. The lithosphere is
(a) hot and plastic; (b) mostly liquid magma; (c) composed mostly of sedimentary rocks; (d) hard, strong rock.

5. The asthenosphere is
(a) hot, plastic, but solid rock; (b) mostly liquid magma; (c) composed mostly of sedimentary rocks; (d) hard, strong solid rock.

6. The center of the Earth's core is
(a) cool and brittle; (b) composed of helium; (c) liquid because the pressure is very high; (d) as hot as the surface of the Sun.

7. At a divergent boundary between spreading tectonic plates in oceanic crust,
(a) one plate subducts beneath the other; (b) rock and magma rise to form the mid-oceanic ridge; (c) rock sinks to form an oceanic trench; (d) rock rises to form continents.

8. The mid-oceanic ridge is elevated above the surrounding sea floor because
(a) it is made of the newest, hottest, and lowest-density lithosphere; (b) it is made of the oldest, coolest, and most dense lithosphere; (c) it is full of gas bubbles; (d) it is very old.

9. Where two plates move horizontally toward each other, they form a
(a) divergent boundary; (b) a rift zone; (c) a convergent boundary; (d) a transform boundary; (e) a mid-oceanic ridge.

10. When a plate carrying continental crust converges with a plate carrying oceanic crust,
(a) the oceanic plate floats above the continental plate (b) the continental plate sinks into the mantle; (c) the oceanic plate sinks beneath the continental plate and dives into the mantle; (d) a divergent boundary forms.

11. Where two plates carrying oceanic crust converge
(a) they form a mid-oceanic ridge; (b) they form a subduction zone and one plate sinks into the mantle; (c) they form a transform boundary; (d) they form a mantle plume.

12. Where two plates carrying continental crust converge
(a) they form a mid-oceanic ridge; (b) both plate stop moving; (c) they form a transform boundary; (d) the continents collide to form a large mountain range.

13. At a transform boundary
(a) one plate subducts into the mantle; (b) a mid-oceanic ridge forms; (c) two plates slide horizontally past each other; (d) volcanic eruptions are common.

14. The San Andreas Fault is an example of
(a) a convergent boundary; (b) a divergent boundary; (c) a transform boundary; (d) a Benioff zone; (e) a rift valley.

15. Tectonic plates typically move at rates of
(a) 1 to 16 millimeters per year; (b) 1 to 16 centimeters per year; (c) 1 to 16 meters per year; (d) 1 to 16 kilometers per year.

16. Tectonic plates move because
(a) the plates are the upper parts of large, deep mantle convection cells; (b) they slide horizontally by isostasy; (c) they are pushed from behind as new oceanic lithosphere forms at a spreading center; (d) volcanic eruptions at the mid-oceanic ridge melt the plates and force them to sink.

17. According to the supercontinent model
(a) at some future time, all continents will join together in a single supercontinent, and plate tectonics activity will cease; (b) continental fragments have migrated around the globe and then

reassembled as a supercontinent at least three times in Earth history; (c) the breakup of a future supercontinent will lead to the destruction of all continental crust in subduction zones; (d) all the geologic provinces in a supercontinent have the same radiometric age.

18. The first supercontinent formed by collisions of microcontinents and island arcs about _____ years ago.
(a) 4.5 billion (b) 3.2 billion (c) 2 to 1.8 billion (d) 5 million (e) 600,000

19. According to the theory of isostasy
(a) the lithosphere is in floating equilibrium on the asthenosphere; (b) plates glide horizontally across the asthenosphere; (c) the asthenosphere is rigid rock; (d) continental crust is denser than oceanic crust.

20. A mantle plume is
(a) a convergent boundary between two plates; (b) a divergent boundary between two plates; (c) a transform boundary between two plates; (d) a rising column of hot, plastic mantle rock.

True or False:

1. The asthenosphere floats on the lithosphere.

2. Oceanic crust ranges from 100 to 200 kilometers in thickness and is composed mostly of granite.

3. The asthenosphere is a rigid, brittle rock layer.

4. The mid-oceanic ridge rises above sea level to form a chain of islands that encircle the Earth like the seam on a baseball.

5. Continental crust is thicker than oceanic crust.

6. About 1 to 2 percent of the asthenosphere is liquid rock.

7. The outer core is liquid.

8. At a divergent boundary, asthenosphere rock oozes upward to fill the gap between separating plates.

9. The mid-oceanic ridge is elevated above surrounding sea floor because it is made of hot and low density lithosphere.

10. The mid-oceanic ridge forms along convergent plate boundaries.

11. If two converging plates are both covered with continental crust, subduction will occur.

12. A plate is a segment of the lithosphere; thus, it includes the uppermost mantle and all of the overlying crust.

13. The oldest continental rocks are 200 million years old whereas the oldest oceanic crust is 3.96 billion years old.

14. Volcanoes, earthquakes and mountain building are consequences of plate movement.

15. According to one hypothesis, lithospheric plates may simply glide downhill on the inclined surface of the asthenosphere.

16. A mantle plume is a vertical column of plastic rock rising from the mantle.

17. According to the theory of isostasy, a dense, heavy portion of the lithosphere would sink into the underlying asthenosphere.

18. Alfred Wegener developed the theory known as continental drift.

Completion:

1. A portion of a plate with continental crust composing its uppermost layer is _____ than one bearing oceanic crust.

2. The _____ is almost 2900 kilometers thick and makes up about 80 percent of the Earth's total volume.

3. The asthenosphere extends to a depth of about _____ kilometers.

4. The _____ is the outermost part of the Earth, including both the uppermost mantle and crust.

5. A divergent plate boundary is also called a/an _____ _____ or a/an _____ _____.

6. Molten rock is called _____.

7. The _____ _____ is an undersea mountain chain that forms at divergent plate boundaries.

8. A continent can be pulled apart at a divergent boundary in a process called _____ _____.

9. A/an _____ _____ is a long, narrow trough in the sea floor formed where a portion of an oceanic plate sinks into the mantle.

10. A/an _____ _____ _____ forms where two plates slide horizontally past each other.

Answers for Chapter 5

Multiple Choice: 1. a; 2. b; 3. b; 4. d; 5. a; 6. d; 7. b; 8. a; 9. c; 10. c; 11. b; 12. d; 13. c; 14. c; 15. b; 16. a; 17. b; 18. c; 19. a; 20. d

True or False: 1. F; 2. F; 3. F; 4. F; 5. T; 6. T; 7. T; 8. T; 9. T; 10. F; 11. F; 12. T; 13. F; 14. T; 15. T; 16. T; 17. T; 18. T

Completion: 1. thicker; 2. mantle; 3. 350; 4. lithosphere; 5. spreading center, rift zone; 6. magma; 7. mid-oceanic ridge; 8. continental rifting; 9. subduction zone; 10. transform plate boundary

CHAPTER 6

Earthquakes and the Earth's Structure

Discussion

This relatively long chapter contains three separate, but related topics, "earthquakes," covered by Sections 6.1 - 6.5, the "use of seismic waves to study the Earth's interior," covered by 6.6, and "Earth magnetism," discussed in the last section.

The plastic behavior of rocks confuses some students because it contradicts their intuitive sense of solid rock. A simple classroom demonstration using road tar can illustrate the point. If a ball of tar is cooled in a freezer and struck with a hammer, it fractures. However, if a tar ball is placed in a wide-necked funnel in a corner of the classroom and left, the tar slowly oozes downward. In a few months a drop will form and if the consistency is right and the temperature high enough, the drop will fall before the final week of the course.

With the chapter on Earthquakes following Plate Tectonics, we have the opportunity to outline earthquake behavior at the three types of plate boundaries (Section 6.3). Thus, our discussion of earthquakes reinforces the students understanding of plate tectonics, and at the same time, the prior knowledge of plate tectonics allows us to discuss earthquake behavior clearly.

Construction codes in earthquake zones are a good example of risk analysis. In making a risk analysis, one must evaluate both the probability of an event and the consequences of the event. Therefore, an area that might be considered "safe" for home construction might not be safe for a nuclear power plant. The difference arises because the consequences of failure of the nuclear power plant are so much greater they are for private homes.

In Section 6.6, we discuss how geologists interpret seismic data to deduce the Earth's structure. Although the Earth's interior was outlined in Chapters 1 and 5, this more detailed look leads the student through the scientific process of data collection and interpretation.

Answers to Discussion Questions

1. 1800 kilometers; 3100 kilometers

2. To measure side to side motion, a weight and pen are mounted on a horizontal rod connected via a flexible fitting to a vertical post mounted on bedrock. The rod is supported by a thin wire attached to the top of the vertical post and the pen writes on a rotating drum that is also connected to bedrock. During an earthquake, the drum and paper move from side to side, but the

horizontal rod and pen tend to remain stationary due to inertia.

3. Northwest Wyoming, in Yellowstone National Park.

4. No, there is no contradiction. In addition to all the factors listed in the text, earthquake mortality depends of people's living habits and luck. In the portion of India struck by the 1993 earthquake, most people live in poorly reinforced masonry homes, which collapsed during the quake. If the quake had occurred during the day when people were outside working in their fields, mortality would have been much lower. In contrast, in the Los Angeles area, most homes did not fail during the quake, but many freeway overpasses collapsed. Thus, if the quake had occurred during rush hour, many more people would have died.

5. As discussed in the text, it is relatively easy to calculate stress accumulation and release along a single fault, but much more difficult to calculate these parameters in a system of many faults lying at different angles. As an exercise, ask students to draw a cross section with intersecting strike-slip and thrust faults. Then ask them to draw arrows indicating presumed distribution of forces as different portions of rock in their diagram move. They will learn that the relationship between force and stress on a given rock is not easy to deduce.

6. It would be an enormously expensive task to close down the city of San Francisco and evacuate its residents.

(upper left hand box) If a predicted earthquake occurs and the city is evacuated, lives will be saved and the geologist who predicted it and recommended evacuation would be applauded.

(upper right hand box) However, if an earthquake is predicted, the city is evacuated, and the quake does not occur, those responsible might be criticized and even sued.

(lower left hand box). If a geologist were to predict a quake, the prediction were ignored, and the quake occurred, everyone would be asked why the prediction was ignored.

(lower right hand box) If an earthquake was not predicted and the city was not evacuated, the lack of prediction would not be particularly noteworthy.

An interesting parallel exists between this problem and industrial accidents. Just before the explosion of the chemical plant in Bhopal, India, the control room operator noted an alarming build up of pressure in the tank where the methyl isocyanate was stored. At this point quick action could have averted disaster, but the operator would have had to destroy the contents of the tank. The operator feared that perhaps the pressure gauge was erratic, and that his superiors would censure him for destroying an expensive batch of chemicals if no emergency existed. So the man did a human thing, he ran out to ask his supervisor. By the time the two men had returned to the control room, it was too late.

In making decisions, you can't always be right, but no one wants to cry wolf unless he or she is certain a real wolf threatens, and often by then it is too late. The point here is that, unfortunately, the penalties for evacuating the city incorrectly are much greater than the rewards for making a correct and life-saving decision.

7. Obviously, there are no correct answers to this question. Existing building codes already establish separate standards for different types of structures. Also the question of an "earthquake-proof" structure is always relative. Do we build structures to resist the largest possible earthquake directly underneath them? In this discussion it is important to remind students about other risks we accept. Many people die in fires; should we also build fireproof homes? What about risks we accept from automobiles and airplanes?

8. For strict codes in the Seattle area: Historical evidence and the presence of the underlying convergent plate boundary indicate that a major earthquake is possible, even likely. If an earthquake were to occur, earthquake-resistant design would save lives.

Against strict codes: While earthquakes have occurred historically, they occur infrequently. Thus there is a low probability that an earthquake will occur during the expected life span of a given building. Therefore the tremendous expense isn't justified.

The same types of arguments apply for Boston and Houston except that these cities don't lie at plate boundaries and therefore earthquake probability is lower. (Boston has experienced some historical quake activity). So once again, the argument centers on balancing cost versus risk, where in these cases, the risk lies on a diminishing scale.

9. The velocity of P waves averages about 6 km/sec in the upper crust (25 km); 7.5 km/sec in the low velocity zone in the upper asthenosphere (200 km); and nearly 10 km/sec in the upper mantle below the asthenosphere (500 km).

10. The Earth's interior is too hot (the outer core is liquid) and a bar magnet could not reverse polarity.

Selected Reading

Some interesting new books on earthquakes are:
Bruce Bolt, *Earthquakes and Geological Discovery*. Holmes, PA: Scientific American, 1993, 229 pages.

Edward A. Keller and Nicholas Pinter, *Active Tectonics: Earthquake, Uplift, and Landscape*. Ontario, Canada: Prentiss Hall, 1996, 338 pages.

Matthys Levy and Mario Salvadori, *Why the Earth Quakes: The Story of Earthquakes and Volcanoes*. New York: Norton, 1995, 215 pages.

For more information about geophysics we recommend:
Ronald T. Merrill, Michael W. McElhinny, and Phillip L. McFadden, *The Magnetic Field of the Earth: Paleomagnetism, the Core, and Deep Mantle*. New York: Academic, 1996, 531 pages.

Shawna Vogel, *Naked Earth, The New Geophysics*. New York: Dutton, 1995, 217 pages.

Discussions of earthquake hazards, predication, and risk analysis are covered in:

Bruce A. Bolt, "Balance of Risk and Benefits in Preparation for Earthquakes." *Science: 251*, January 11, 1991, pp. 169-174.

Leon Reiter, *Earthquake Hazard Analysis*. New York: Columbia University Press, 1991, 254 pages.

Herbert Tiedemann, *Earthquakes and Volcanic Eruptions: A Handbook on Risk Assessment*. Zurich: Swiss Reinsurance Company, 1992, 951 pages.

A review of earthquake hazards in California is available in:
James F. Dolan et al., "Prospects for Larger or More Frequent Earthquakes in the Los Angeles Metropolitan Region." *Science,267*, 1995, pp. 199-214.

Chapter 6 Test

Multiple Choice:

1. When solid rock can deforms and does not return to its original shape it has undergone
(a) elastic deformation; (b) plastic deformation; (c) liquefaction; (d) brittle fracture.

2. The edges of two adjacent tectonic plates may show no relative movement for hundreds of years while the interiors of the plates move because
(a) rock is brittle; (b) rock stretches or compresses; (c) earthquakes rarely occur at tectonic plate boundaries; (d) volcanic eruptions introduce hot lava that welds the sides of the fault together.

3. A P, or primary, wave
(a) forms by alternate compression and expansion of rock; (b) travels much faster than the speed of sound; (c) passes through both solids and liquids; (d) all of the above; (e) none of the above.

4. An S or shear waves
(a) moves only through solids; (b) is slower than a P-wave; (c) travels at 3 to 4 km/second in the crust; (d) all of the above; (e) none of the above.

5. The moment magnitude scale
(a) is an accurate indicator of the energy released during an earthquake; (b) can be used to locate the earthquake epicenter; (c) is calculated from the height of the largest earthquake wave recorded on a specific type of seismograph; (d) is measured by recording the amount of structural damage in an area.

6. To measure the distance from a recording station to an earthquake epicenter, geologists
(a) measure the magnitude of an earthquake; (b) measure the refraction of P and S waves; (c) study the amplitude of the largest earthquake waves; (d) compare the time interval between the arrival of P and S waves with a time-travel curve.

7. The San Andreas fault zone is an example of
(a) an earthquake zone at a transform plate boundary; (b) a Benioff zone; (c) a deep focus earthquake zone; (d) an earthquake zone at a subduction plate boundary; (e) an earthquake at a divergent plate boundary.

8. The Northridge earthquake of January 1994

(a) occurred at a subduction zone adjacent to a transform plate boundary; (b) occurred directly over the San Andreas Fault; (c) occurred on a thrust fault adjacent to the San Andreas Fault; (d) was triggered by a body of hot rising magma.

9. The earthquakes caused when a subducting plate sinks into the mantle
(a) concentrate along the upper part of the sinking plate; (b) concentrate in the asthenosphere adjacent to the sinking plate; (c) are very shallow earthquakes; (d) occur only in conjunction with volcanic activity along the subduction zone.

10. The major 1995 earthquake in Kobe, Japan occurred
(a) near a transform plate boundary; (b) at a divergent plate boundary; (c) in a plate interior; (d) near a subduction zone.

11. Earthquakes occur along the mid-oceanic ridge because
(a) the subducting plate scrapes along the lower crust; (b) two plates slip horizontally past one another; (c) blocks of oceanic crust drop downward as the rift valley opens; (d) large submarine landslides occur on the landward edge of the subduction zone.

12. If you were mayor of Los Angeles, what would be a reasonable, cost-effective approach to saving lives if a large earthquake were to strike?
(a) Evacuate the city immediately after any sequence of small quakes; (b) pass a building code that would mandate that every structure be able to withstand a magnitude 8 quake directly under its foundation; (c) gradually strengthen building codes with an emphasis on selected structures such as nuclear power plants; (d) attempt to weld the San Andreas Fault together with concrete and steel reinforcement.

13. No S waves pass through the center of the Earth because
(a) the asthenosphere is liquid; (b) the outer core is liquid; (c) S waves travel only through liquids; (d) S waves refract at the mantle-core boundary.

14. Geologists learned that the outer core is liquid because
(a) S waves refract at the mantle-core boundary; (b) P waves refract at the mantle-core boundary; (c) S waves do not travel through the outer core; (d) P waves do not travel through the outer core.

15. The likely source of the Earth's magnetism is
(a) its revolution around the Sun; (b) a permanent magnet within the Earth's core; (c) the flow of electrons and positive metal ions in the outer core; (d) convection currents in the mantle.

True or False:

1. Where two tectonic plates move past one another, rock near the plate boundary often stretches and stores elastic energy.

2. P waves in the Earth travel more than ten times slower than the speed of sound in air.

3. Surface waves travel more slowly than either type of body wave.

4. The largest earthquakes ever observed had magnitudes of 8.5 to 8.7, about 900 times greater than the energy released by the Hiroshima bomb.

5. The New Madrid earthquake of 1811 occurred at a plate boundary.

6. Earthquakes occur in the Pacific Northwest because a transform plate boundary passes through the region.

7. Only deep earthquakes occur along the mid-oceanic ridge.

8. Earthquakes never occur in plate interiors.

9. P and S waves travel through all types of material.

10. P and S waves travel more rapidly in the crust than they do in the mantle.

Completion:

1. A/an _____ is a sudden motion or trembling of the Earth.

2. When rock retains its new shape (without fracturing) after stress has been removed, it has undergone _____ _____.

3. The initial rupture point of an earthquake is called the _____.

4. The fastest seismic waves are called _____ _____.

5. _____ _____ waves can travel through solids but not through liquids.

6. Earthquakes are detected and measured with a device called a _____.

7. A type of continuous, snail-like movement that occurs along the San Andreas Fault is called _____ _____.

8. _____ are small earthquakes that precede a large quake by an interval ranging from a few seconds to a few weeks.

9. A/an _____ is a sea wave generated by an underwater earthquake.

10. A wave _____ and sometimes reflects as it passes from one transmitting medium into another.

Answers for Chapter 6

Multiple Choice: 1. b; 2. b; 3. c; 4. d; 5. a; 6. d; 7. a; 8. c; 9. a; 10. d; 11. c; 12. c; 13. b; 14. c; 15. c

True or False: 1. T; 2. F; 3. T; 4. T; 5. F; 6. F; 7. F; 8. F; 9. F; 10. F

Completion: 1. earthquake; 2. plastic deformation; 3. focus; 4. P waves; 5. S waves; 6. seismograph; 7. fault creep; 8. Foreshocks; 9. tsunami; 10. refracts

CHAPTER 7

Volcanoes and Plutons

Discussion

In the introduction to Chapter 7, we describe the effects of some recent volcanic eruptions on humans. We then describe the processes that form magma, the tectonic environments in which magma originates, and the respective origins of the two most common types of magma: basaltic and granitic. In Section 7.3, we discuss magma behavior and explain why basaltic magma typically erupts onto the Earth's surface to form volcanic rocks, whereas intermediate and granitic magma commonly solidifies within the crust to form plutonic rocks. We stress that both silica and water content exerts important effects on magma behavior.

Section 7.4 describes plutons and other plutonic rock bodies, and Section 7.5 describes volcanic processes, landforms, and rocks. In Section 7.6 we describe the violent caldera eruptions that occur when granitic and intermediate magmas rise close to the Earth's surface rather than solidifying at depth. The Yellowstone and Long Valley-Mammoth Mountain environments are used as examples. The chapter continues with a discussion of risk assessment of volcanic regions, using the 1980 Mount St. Helens and the 1997 Montserrat disasters as examples. Section 7.8 describes the relationships between volcanic eruptions and global climate change.

Answers to Discussion Questions

1. In the absence of water, increasing pressure raises the melting point of rock because a rock must expand in order to melt. For the same reason, decreasing pressure lowers the solidification temperature of magma (melting point and solidification temperature are opposite sides of the same coin, if partial melting is ignored). The explanation is the same for both basaltic and granitic magma, if both are dry.

However, most basaltic magma is nearly dry, whereas most granitic magma contains up to 10 percent water. In this case, pressure effects are different, because water depresses melting points, and high pressure increases the solubility of water in magma. Thus, high pressure allows more water to dissolve in wet granitic magma, depressing its melting point. In contrast, high pressure raises the melting point of dry basaltic magma. The contrast in water contents of the two types of magma accounts largely for the fact that much basaltic magma rises to erupt from volcanoes (because its solidification temperature drops as it rises into lower pressure zones). In contrast, much granitic magma loses water as it rises because of decreasing pressure, and thus, its solidification temperature rises, causing it to solidify within the crust.

2. A subduction zone is the only one of the three major magma-producing tectonic environments in which water is added to hot rock (by dewatering of the sinking slab and addition of that water into the upper asthenosphere of the adjacent abducted plate). Both other environments - mantle plumes and spreading centers - have no source of large amounts of available water.

3. If the sill cooled at depth, a coarse grained intrusive rock would form whereas extrusive rocks are commonly fine-grained or porphyritic. If present, vesicles tend to be more abundant in the upper parts of a sill, but they are commonly abundant near the tops of flows, too. Additionally, many lava flows have autobrecciated bases and tops; sills do not. Sills may have chilled margins and produce contact metamorphism at both contacts. Paleosols and other clues provide additional evidence when present.

4. Volcanoes form under a variety of conditions, depending on the temperature, pressure, and composition of the interior of a planet. On Triton, the largest of Neptune's moons, flat plains are believed to be methane lava flows. Obviously methane lava (melting point -182°C) forms under different conditions from basaltic lava, but the concepts are the same. Magma forms when material in the interior of a planet is heated or when its pressure or composition are altered so that it melts. In order to learn more about the geology of other planets, you would need data on the composition of the lava, its temperature, the extent of tectonic activity on the planet, etc.

5. Volcanic eruptions commonly form symmetrical, conical mountains with gentle to moderate slopes; the flanks can then be steepened by weathering and erosion. However, some volcanoes are asymmetrical because the eruption is lateral. The 1980 eruption of Mount St. Helens is one such example. Magma composition also plays an important role in determining the steepness of a volcano. Lava plateaus and shield volcanoes form mostly from basaltic magma with low viscosity, whereas steeper composite volcanoes and cinder cones form from more viscous intermediate to felsic magma. Extremely steep spines and domes of intermediate to felsic composition may rise in the craters of some volcanoes.

6. Mount St. Helens has erupted more frequently but less catastrophically than the Yellowstone region. If you lived very close (5 km), the high frequency of eruption would make Mount St. Helens the more dangerous location. Fifty kilometers is probably close enough to Mount St. Helens to be dangerous. The blast from the 1980 eruption blew down trees 25 kilometers from the vent, and ash flows and mudflows followed river valleys for tens of kilometers. Therefore, even at 50 kilometers, the danger from Mount St. Helens is probably greater than from the Yellowstone region. However, another cataclysmic Yellowstone caldera eruption would initiate fires and eject ash that could cause damage and loss of life 500 kilometers away. Thus, while the

probability that an eruption will occur is lower, there is a finite danger in living 500 kilometers from Yellowstone.

7. The answers to this question depend on the locality of the students' location. The maps and information provided in the chapter are sufficient to answer the question.

8. Effects of a large caldera eruption on humans fall into three categories, local, regional, and global. Local effects include damage resulting from an explosive blast, from ash flows, and from mud and debris flows. In addition, debris from such an eruption commonly interrupts drainage patterns, causing floods and additional debris flows. Proximity of towns to a caldera eruption controls whether or not large numbers of people are effected by such an event. In addition, ash flows and debris flows tend to follow stream valleys, so population density in valleys downstream from such an eruption is an important consideration.

Regional effects include the settling out of volcanic ash, which has health effects, disrupts normal life and commerce patterns, and damages machinery. But these effects last only for a short time, until most of the ash has fallen to Earth. Global effects result largely from fine ash and volcanic gases rising into the upper atmosphere, where they can affect climate for years after the eruption. It may be useful to recall that some geologists attribute mass extinctions to such volcanic events.

The probability that a large caldera eruption will occur in the future approaches 100 percent; such eruptions have occurred throughout geologic time. The probability that such an eruption will occur within the next 10 or 100 years is low, however. The average frequency of the past 3 Yellowstone eruptions is about one every 0.6 million years. Other large caldera systems seem to erupt repeatedly, but with similarly long quiet intervals separating major eruptions.

9. Interactions among volcanic eruptions and other tectonic processes, and the biosphere, the hydrosphere, the atmosphere and the geosphere are the topics of the Opening Essays to Units I through V. They are: Unit I "Earth Rocks, Earth History, and Mass Extinctions"; Unit II "Plate Tectonics and Earth Systems"; Unit III "The Evolution of the Oceans, the Atmosphere, and Life"; Unit IV "Flowers Bloomed on Earth While Venus Boiled and Mars Froze"; Unit V "Origin of Iron Ore and the Evolution of Earth's Atmosphere, Biosphere, and Oceans". In addition, Unit VI, "Human Population and Alteration of Earth Systems" discusses impacts of human activities on Earth systems. We hope this and similar discussion questions will lead students to read those essays.

Selected Reading

General books on volcanoes and eruptions are:
Richard V. Fisher, Grant Heiken, and Jeffrey B. Hulen, *Volcanoes, Crucibles of Change*. Princeton, NJ: Princeton University Press, 1998.

James F. Luhr and Tom Simkin with Margaret Cuasay, *Paricutin: The Volcano Born in a Mexican Cornfield*. Phoenix: Geoscience Press, 1993.

Alwyn Scarth, *Volcanoes*. Houston: UCL/Texas A&M University Press, 1994, 273 pages.

Tom Simkin and Lee Siebert, *Volcanoes of the World Second Edition*. Missoula, MT: Geoscience Press, 1995, 368 pages.

Discussions of volcanoes as geologic hazards and how to deal with them are found in:
Herbert Tiedemann, *Earthquakes and Volcanic Eruptions: A Handbook on Risk Assessment*. Zurich: Swiss Reinsurance Company, 1992, 951 pages.

Bill McGuire, Christopher Kilburn, and John Murray, *Monitoring Active Volcanoes: Strategies, Procedures and Techniques*. Berkeley, CA: UCL Press, 1995, 421 pages.

The effect of a volcano on an ecosystem is discussed in:
Ian Thorton, *Krakatau: The Destruction and Reassembly of an Island Ecosystem*. Boston: Harvard University Press, 1996, 346 pages.

General discussions of plutonic and volcanic rocks and their geologic environments are found in:
Donald Hyndman, *Petrology of Igneous and Metamorphic Rocks, 2nd Ed.* New York: McGraw-Hill, 1985.

Calderas and ash-flow tuffs are discussed in:
Grant Heiken, Fraser Goff, Jamie N. Gardner, W. S. Baldridge, J. B. Hulen, Dennis L. Nielson, David Vaniman: The Valles/Toledo Caldera Complex, Jemez Volcanic Field. *Annual Review of Earth and Planetary Sciences*:18 (27), 1990.

John B. Rundle and David P. Hill: The Geophysics of a Restless Caldera -- Long Valley, California. *Annual Review of Earth and Planetary Sciences 16*:(251), 1988.

Chapter 7 Test

Multiple Choice:

1. Which of the following processes causes melting of the asthenosphere and the generation of magma?
(a) removal of water; (b) decreasing pressure; (c) decreasing temperature; (d) all of the above.

2. Which of the following tectonic environments does not generate large quantities of magma?
(a) spreading centers; (b) mantle plumes; (c) subduction zones; (d) transform boundaries.

3. The "ring of fire", a zone of concentrated volcanic activity encircling the Pacific Ocean basin, is located adjacent to
(a) subduction zones; (b) rift zones; (c) the mid-oceanic ridge; (d) a lava plateau; (e) the San Andreas fault.

4. Granite is common in continents because
(a) the asthenosphere is mostly granite; (b) the lower lithosphere is mostly granite; (c) basaltic magma rises into granitic continental crust, melting it to form granitic magma; (d) granite melts at a higher temperature than basalt.

5. Basalt magma has a _____ melting temperature compared to granitic magma.
(a) lower (b) higher (c) equal

6. Typical granitic magma contains _____ silica and _____ water than typical basaltic magma.
(a) more, less; (b) more, more; (c) less, less; (d) less, more.

7. Magma with a high water content has a greater tendency to _____ in the crust, compared with magma with a lower water content.
(a) solidify; (b) remain liquid; (c) metamorphose; (d) erupt to form volcanoes.

8. The magma type that most commonly rises to the Earth's surface to erupt from a volcano is
(a) granitic magma; (b) potassium-rich magma; (c) basaltic magma; (d) plutonic magma.

9. Most basaltic magma erupts at the Earth's surface because
(a) it contains little water; (b) it contains huge amounts of water; (c) it is more viscous than

granitic magma; (e) it has a high silica content than granitic magma.

10. Loss of water from rising granitic magma causes it to
(a) erupt at the surface; (b) solidify within the crust; (c) remain liquid until it reaches the Earth's surface; (d) none of the above.

11. A pluton with an outcrop area of more than 100 square kilometers is a
(a) volcanic neck; (b) batholith; (c) stock; (d) dike; (e) volcano.

12. The immense quantities of granitic magma that form batholiths commonly form
(a) within the deep sea floor; (b) at subduction zones; (c) at the Mid-Atlantic ridge; (d) at transform faults

13. As lava cools and solidifies from the surface down, cracks frequently grow downward through the rock. Such cracks are called
(a) batholiths; (b) sills; (c) columnar joints; (d) stocks; (e) plutons.

14. Lava with a jagged, rubbly surface is
(a) pahoehoe; (b) aa; (c) granitic; (d) plutonic; (e) cosmic.

15. Pillow lava forms as pillow-shaped lenses because it
(a) erupts under water; (b) usually has a granitic composition; (c) is abundant in granitic crust; (d) is rare in oceanic crust.

16. Pyroclastic bombs, cinders, and ash
(a) erupt explosively from volcanoes; (b) flow gently from volcanoes; (c) solidify within the crust as irregularly-shaped plutons; (d) occur as dikes and sills intruded into country rock.

17. The gentlest, least catastrophic type of volcanic eruption occurs when magma is so fluid that it simply oozes from cracks to form
(a) flood basalts; (b) caldera eruptions; (c) cinder cones; (d) composite volcanoes; (e) nuees ardentes.

18. If basaltic magma is too viscous to form a lava plateau, but still quite fluid, it heaps up slightly forming
(a) flood basalts; (b) pillow lava; (c) cinder cones; (d) shield volcanoes; (e) nuee ardente.

19. A composite cone

(a) is usually active for only a short time; (b) forms by repeated lava flows and pyroclastic eruptions over a long time; (c) forms by pyroclastic eruptions only; (d) forms in a single, cataclysmic event.

20. Which magma type erupts most violently?
(a) basaltic; (b) Hawaiian; (c) Icelandic; (d) granitic.

21. A caldera eruption commonly occurs when
(a) water-saturated basaltic magma rises; (b) dry basaltic magma rises; (c) water-saturated granitic magma rises; (d) relatively dry granitic magma rises.

22. When an ash flow comes to a stop, most of the gas escapes into the atmosphere, leaving behind a chaotic mixture of volcanic ash and rock fragments called
(a) ash-flow basalt; (b) pillow lava; (c) a submarine volcano; (d) a shield volcano; (e) ash-flow tuff.

23. A caldera is a
(a) gently sloping mountain formed by low-viscosity magma pouring from a central vent; (b) a steep conical mountain formed by repeated lava flows and pyroclastic eruptions; (c) a circular depression formed as the roof of a magma chamber collapses during an eruption (d) a broad, flat lava plateau formed by fluid magma.

24. Yellowstone Park is an example of three overlapping
(a) shield volcanoes; (b) mantle plumes; (c) calderas; (d) lava plateaus; (e) composite cones.

True or False:

1. Granitic crust forms at the mid-oceanic ridge.

2. Granitic magma has longer chains of silicate tetrahedra than basaltic magma.

3. If magma contains large amounts of water, the water escapes as the magma rises and the solidification temperature rises, causing the magma to solidify

4. A sill forms when magma oozes between layers of country rock.

5. Aa lava cools and stiffens as it flows, forming basalt with smooth, glassy-surfaced, wrinkled,

or "ropy" ridges.

6. The gentlest, least catastrophic type of volcanic eruption occurs when magma is so fluid that it simply oozes from cracks as a nuee ardente.

7. A cinder cone is usually active for only a short period of time because once the gas escapes, the driving force behind the eruption is removed.

8. A volcanic pipe is a conduit filled with the last bit of magma that solidified within it.

9. The granitic magmas that do rise to the surface probably start out with more water than normal granitic magma.

10. The periodicity of Yellowstone eruptions, the presence of shallow magma, and the well-known tendency of magma of this type to erupt multiple times all suggest that a fourth eruption may occur.

11. Geologists can identify regions with a high risk of volcanic eruption, but have never been able to offer an accurate short term prediction of a volcanic eruption.

12. When Mount St. Helens erupted in 1980, it released all its steam and magma and is not expected to erupt again.

Completion:

1. Long chains of silicate tetrahedra form in magma with _____ composition.

2. Granitic magma contains up to _____ percent water.

3. A granitic pluton that is exposed for more than 100 square kilometers is called a/an

_____.

4. A _____ is a tabular or sheet-like intrusive rock that cuts across sedimentary layers.

5. If lava solidifies before the gas in it escapes, the bubbles are preserved as holes called

_____.

6. _____ _____ consists of tiny fragments of glass that formed when liquid magma exploded into the air.

7. A _____ _____ is a volcanic mountain formed by fluid basaltic magma, whose sides generally slope 6° to 12° from the horizontal.

8. Explosively erupted rock particles or magma form _____ rock.

9. When large blobs of molten lava spin through the air, they solidify to form _____ _____.

10. A/an _____ _____ is a small, symmetrical, generally short-lived volcano, made up of pyroclastic fragments blasted out of a central vent.

11. Mount St. Helens and Mount Rainier are examples of _____ _____.

12. About 70 percent of the Earth's volcanic activity, except for that at the mid-oceanic ridge system, occurs along a circle of subduction zones in the Pacific Ocean called the _____ _____ _____.

13. A volcanic rock that is so full of small gas bubbles that it floats is called _____.

14. A tough, hard rock that forms when a hot ash flow partly or completely melts before it solidifies is _____ _____.

15. The circular depression left when the roof of a magma chamber collapses is called a/an _____.

Answers for Chapter 7

Multiple Choice: 1. b; 2. d; 3. a; 4. c; 5. b; 6. a; 7. a; 8. c; 9. a; 10. b; 11. b; 12. b; 13. c; 14. b; 15. a; 16. a; 17. a; 18. d; 19. b; 20. d; 21. d; 22. e; 23. c; 24. c.

True or False: 1. F; 2. T; 3. T; 4. T; 5. F; 6. F; 7. T; 8. T; 9. F; 10. T; 11. F; 12. F

Completion: 1. granitic; 2. 10; 3. batholith; 4. dike; 5. vesicles; 6. Volcanic ash; 7. shield volcano; 8. pyroclastic, the particles are called ash, bomb, cinders, etc.; 9. volcanic bombs; 10. cinder cone; 11. composite cones or stratovolcanoes; 12. ring of fire; 13. pumice; 14. welded tuff; 15. caldera

CHAPTER 8

Geologic Structures, Mountain Ranges, and Continents

Discussion

In this chapter we introduce the fundamental concepts of structural geology. These concepts are presented in the context of the processes that form most geological structures: The development of orogens, or mountain building. The plate tectonics concepts discussed in previous chapters are applied to the building of mountain ranges.

Structural geology is a fascinating and informative branch of geology. We feel that the important structural concepts for an introductory course are few and simple: Plate movements generate tectonic stress, particularly near plate boundaries. The stress, in turn, causes elastic, plastic, and/or brittle deformation in rocks. Deformation occurs as folds, faults, and joints. Relationships among types of plate boundaries, types of stress, and geologic structures are described.

Intuition leads students, and many of us geologists, to conclude that a simple relationship must exist between each of the three types of plate boundaries and the type of tectonic stress that predominate at each: rift boundaries seem to logically involve extensional stress; transform boundaries should produce shear stress; and convergent boundaries should involve compressive stress. We point out that this is commonly the case, particularly for rift and transform boundaries. However, convergent or subduction boundaries often are accompanied by regional extension. As Warren Hamilton frequently observes, much of western South America seems currently to be under extension, and simultaneously is a subduction margin.

After introducing geological structures and the general idea that mountain chains form at tectonic plate boundaries, we use these ideas to describe the origins of two of the Earth's greatest mountain chains: the Andes and the Himalayas. Nearly all students have some geographic familiarity with both mountain chains. Their respective origins and the fact that both mountain chains are still in the process of rising today are intrinsically interesting to most students. Further, reading about the geological processes that formed these mountain chains strongly reinforces students' understanding of the processes themselves.

In this edition, we added two new sections: In Section 8.7, "Mountains and Earth Systems" we stress the Earth systems theme by explaining that, while mountains are lifted by tectonic forces, they then interact with the hydrosphere, atmosphere, and biosphere. Also new to this edition, we added a short section on the origin of continents because this topic is an interesting area of current research.

Answers to Discussion Questions

1. Divergent plate boundaries, whether in oceanic or continental lithosphere, are characterized by extension, normal faulting, grabens, and basaltic volcanism.

The dominant feature of a transform plate boundary is a system of huge, lithosphere-deep, strike-slip faults. Secondary stress generated along these faults creates both compressive and extensional features in relatively small crustal blocks adjacent to the main faults. Basaltic volcanism may occur if the transform is "leaky."

All three types of stress, compression, extension, and shear, may occur at convergent boundaries, at different times or in different places at the same time. Compressional stress can be dominant where an island arc docks against a continental margin, or where two continents collide. It may also occur at a continental margin when convergence rates are high. Compression occurs within the subduction complex adjacent a trench. Extension can also accompany plate convergence, as seems to be the case currently in parts of the Andes. If subduction occurs along a relatively high density, cool, old, portion of a plate, little or no compression should be expected in the subducting plate except in the vicinity of the subduction complex, and extension is likely. Shearing occurs along oblique subduction zones. Horizontal shearing certainly occurs in subduction complexes, as a result of compression.

2. All three of these features are formed by compression.

3. Most continental mountain chains form at convergent plate boundaries either where subduction of oceanic lithosphere occurs at a continental margin (the Andes along the west coast of South America), or where two continents collide (the Himalayas). Subduction generates huge quantities of magma. Continent-continent collisions generate underthrusting, folding, and resultant uplift. As a result of these processes, immense mountain chains such as the Andes and the Himalayas rise near convergent plate boundaries.

Continental rifting results from development of a divergent plate boundary in continental crust. High escarpments result from normal faulting, and volcanic mountains form in such environments, as in the East African Rift. Generally, little folding or deformation other than normal faulting occur in continental rifts because the stress is mainly extensional.

A transform plate boundary exists along the San Andreas fault in western California. Here, small, folded and faulted mountain ranges are rising along the fault zone. Somewhat similar ranges are forming along the great strike-slip faults in Tibet, China, and Mongolia, north of the Himalayas. Although this region is not a transform plate boundary, the huge strike-slip faults generate similar tectonic forces and structures.

4. Extensional forces develop in a compressional environment when portions of the crust ooze out under their own weight. This can happen if a mountain becomes too steep and heavy, as in the Himalayas and the Andes. It has also occurred during the development of the North American Cordillera. Extension occurred as the rate of plate convergence slowed down and the warm thick crust spread out like a mound of homey on a table top. Extension also occurred in the Basin and Range of North America as motion along the San Andreas fault exerted frictional drag against the western margin of the continent.

5. Many mountain ranges are formed by subduction of a oceanic plate with a continental plate (sometimes followed by continent-continent collision). Sediment collects and sedimentary rocks form in the shallow sea along the continental margin or on the deep sea floor. These sediments and rocks may be scraped off and forced upward during formation of a subduction complex. Sedimentary rocks of the subduction complex are also uplifted as subduction consumes the oceanic crust and two continents collide.

      Sediment also accumulates from eroding mountains and in the great time of mountain formation, these sediments may lithify to form sedimentary rocks that then become part of the mountains.

6. The Urals were formed by convergence between a plate carrying oceanic crust and one carrying continental crust, followed by continent-continent collision. Thus the mountains formed along a continental margin that became a continental interior as two contents fused.

7. Early development of the Himalayas must have been similar to the present stage of development of the Andes. Major differences developed later, when India collided with southern Asia. That collision transformed the Himalayan region from an Andean-type margin to a continental collision plate margin. Thus, 60 million years ago the Himalayan region may have been very similar to the modern Andes.

8. Large amounts of granitic rocks are found on the Tibetan side of the Himalayas. They are located on the northern side of the continental suture and the early subduction zones that preceded the continental collision. The southern side of the suture is characterized by folded and faulted sedimentary rocks. The igneous rocks concentrate on the northern side of the suture because subduction that preceded the continental collision involved oceanic lithosphere diving northward beneath the southern margin of Tibet.

9. Subduction and mountain building began to form the Himalayan chain about 80 million years ago. If the Himalayas had risen at a rate of 1 centimeter per year for 80 million years, they would now be 800,000 meters high. In fact the highest peaks are a little over 8000 meter, 1/100 this

calculated height. Clearly, mountain building is not a steady linear process, nor would we expect it to be. Different process formed the Himalaya at different times; plates have moved at different speeds. In addition, abundant evidence from earthquakes and volcanoes indicate that rock slippage and magma movement often occur in alternating periods of activity and quiescence. Most evidence indicates that today, the Himalayas are undergoing rapid isostatic rebound in response to rapid erosion.

10. Sea floor rocks subduct back into the mantle after about 200 million years. Old rocks are found in portions of the craton because these regions have not been subject to tectonic change for billions of years. While some mountain ranges, such as the Andes, are composed mainly of relatively young rocks, other mountains such as the Tetons in Wyoming contain abundant old rocks. The age of rocks in mountains depends on the mechanism of mountain formation.

11. The classic example of this scenario occurs when people cut forested hillsides for agriculture. When the trees are cut, the hillsides are more prone to landslides that in turn may destroy homes and villages. At the same time, after forested hillsides are logged, stream flow increases during the rainy seasons and decreases during the dry seasons, so flood and drought become more pronounced downstream.

12. As explained in the text, mountains affect climate because high elevations are cooler than lowlands, and because moisture condenses from rising air to form abundant precipitation. Rainfall collects in streams that erode mountainsides. If the mountains are cool and wet enough, glaciers form, and glaciers also erode landscapes. Air cools and precipitation forms very rapidly --within hours-- as it encounters a mountain. However, erosion rates occur much more slowly, wearing mountain ranges down over tens of millions of years.

Selected Reading

Two general references on mountain formation are:
A. J. Gerrard, *Mountain Environments: An Examination of the Physical Geography of Mountains.* Cambridge: MIT Press, 1990, 317 pages.

Jack D. Ives, ed., *Mountains*. New York: Rodale Press, 1994, 160 pages.

Continents and their formation are discussed in:
Derek Blundell, Roy Freeman, and Stephan Mueller, eds., *A Continent Revealed*. New York: Cambridge University Press, 1992, 288 pages.

Eldrige M. Moores, ed., *Shaping the Earth: Tectonics of Continents and Oceans*. New York: W. H. Freeman, 1990, 206 pages.

Brian F. Windley, *The Evolving Continents, Third Edition*. New York: John Wiley, 1995, 526 pages.

An excellent review article on the formation of continental crust is:
Roberta L. Rudnick, "Making Continental Crust." *Nature*. Volume 378, December 7, 1995. pg. 571.

Chapter 8 Test

Multiple Choice:

1. The Mississippi River delta lies in a plate interior. Sediment within the delta, buried by a few kilometers of younger sediment on top, is deformed by
(a) confining stress; (c) compressive stress; (d) tensional stress; (e) shear stress.

2. A cool rock near the Earth's surface is more likely to _____ than a similar rock that is hot and under great pressure.
(a) deform plastically; (b) undergo brittle fracture; (c) undergo pressure release melting; (d) metamorphose.

3. Rock in the Himalaya that is caught at the junction of two converging plates is deformed by
(a) confining stress; (c) compressive stress; (d) tensional stress; (e) shear stress.

4. A fold in a rock indicates that
(a) the rock has deformed by brittle fracture; (b) the rock is under extensional stress; (c) the rock has been subjected to confining stress; (d) the rock has deformed in a plastic manner.

5. An anticline
(a) always forms mountain peaks; (b) always forms mountain valleys; (c) forms as a part of a sequence of folds during crustal extension; (d) is the portion of a fold that arches upward.

6. A reverse fault occurs as a result of
(a) crustal extension; (b) crustal shortening; (c) the hanging wall moving downward relative to the footwall; (d) plastic behavior of rock.

7. A wedge-shaped block of rock that drops downward between a pair of normal faults is
(a) a horst; (b) a anticline; (c) a syncline; (d) a graben; (e) a hanging wall.

8. Rock often moves repeatedly along many faults because
(a) tectonic stress commonly continues to be active in the same place over long periods of time; (b) all faults lie along tectonic plate boundaries; (c) faulting is a strong indication that rock in the region is distorting plastically; (d) faults always lie over shallow bodies of hot magma.

9. Normal faults, grabens, and horsts are common

(a) where the crust is being pulled apart; (b) at convergent boundaries; (c) at hot spots; (d) along transform plate boundaries.

10. The San Andreas fault is an example of a
(a) reverse fault; (b) normal fault; (c) strike-slip fault; (d) tight fold.

11. Where two oceanic plates converge, one sinks beneath the other and dives into the mantle forming
(a) a mid-ocean ridge; (b) an Andean margin; (c) an island arc; (d) an accreted terrain.

12. A subduction complex
(a) is a layer of volcanic rocks that erupts during subduction in an ocean basin; (b) is formed from sedimentary rock eroded from young mountains in a island arc; (c) is formed from slices of rock and sediment scraped off the ocean floor during subduction; (d) characteristically forms in the interior of a tectonic plate.

13. The Andes Mountains were formed
(a) by convergence of two plates each carrying oceanic crust; (b) by convergence of two plates each carrying continental crust; (c) by convergence of a plate carrying oceanic crust with a plate carrying continental crust; (d) at a divergent plate boundary where oceanic crust is separating from continental crust.

14. When the Andes became sufficiently high and heavy, weak soft rock oozed outward under its weight. This oozing
(a) formed a great belt of thrust faults and folds; (b) formed horsts and grabens on the west side of the range; (c) formed massive quantities of igneous rocks; (d) slowed the rate of subduction and reduced volcanic activity throughout the range.

15. The Himalayas were formed by
(a) convergence of an oceanic plate with a continental plate, followed by continent-continent collision; (b) convergence of two oceanic plates followed by continent-continent collision; (c) continent-continent collision followed by convergence of an oceanic plate with a continental plate; (d) continent-continent collision followed by convergence of two oceanic plates.

16. The underthrusting of India beneath Tibet
(a) initiated an intense period of volcanic activity; (b) sheared the underside of the Tibetan crust so that today the Himalayas ride on a thin crust; (c) doubled the thickness of continental crust; (d) diverted the India plate, creating a transform fault with numerous earthquakes.

17. During Archean time
(a) there were no continents, just a global ocean; (b) continental crust covered the entire globe and there were no ocean basins; (c) the Earth was probably dotted with numerous small continents and island arcs; (d) the Earth was so hot that the entire surface was molten.

18. Partial melting of the Earth's earliest primordial crust
(a) formed sedimentary rocks; (b) formed a basaltic crust that was richer in silica than the mantle; (c) formed granitic continents; (d) occurred mainly at transform plate boundaries.

True or False:

1. Rocks trapped between converging plates carrying continental crust commonly bend and fracture.

2. If tectonic forces fracture the Earth's crust, rocks on opposite sides of the fracture may move past each other to create a fault.

3. If tectonic forces stretch the crust over a large area, many thrust faults may develop, allowing numerous grabens to settle downward along the faults.

4. Where two continental plates converge, compressional forces squeeze rocks, forming folds and reverse and thrust faults.

5. The western Aleutian Islands and most of the island chains of the southwestern Pacific basin occur along strike-slip faults.

6. The Andes developed from a convergence between a tectonic plate carrying oceanic crust and another carrying continental crust.

7. The modern Himalayas continue to grow as a plate carrying oceanic crust subducts beneath a plate carrying continental crust.

8. The Himalayas are rising as frequent volcanic eruptions add to the thickness of the continental crust.

9. All of the Earth's continental land masses formed by the end of Archean time.

10. According to one model vertical or plume tectonics dominated Earth geology in Archean time.

Completion:

1. _____ _____ compresses rocks but does not distort them.

2. A/an _____ _____ is any feature produced by rock deformation.

3. A circular or elliptical anticlinal structure is called a/an _____.

4. In a reverse fault the hanging wall has moved _____ relative to the footwall.

5. The term _____ refers to the process of mountain building.

6. The western Aleutian Islands are an example of a/an _____ _____.

7. The _____ are a relatively narrow mountain chain on the west coast of South America composed predominantly of volcanic and plutonic rocks formed by subduction at a continental margin.

8. During the formation of the Himalayas, the leading edge of India began to slide under Tibet in a process called _____.

Answers for Chapter 8

Multiple Choice: 1. a; 2. b; 3. c; 4. d; 5. d; 6. b; 7. d; 8. a; 9. a; 10. c; 11. c; 12. c; 13. c; 14. a; 15. a; 16. c; 17. c; 18. b

True of False: 1. T; 2. T; 3. F; 4. T; 5. F; 6. T; 7. F; 8. F; 9. F; 10. T

Completion: 1. confining stress; 2. geologic structure; 3. dome; 4. up or upward; 5. orogeny; 6. island arc; 7. Andes; 8. underthrusting

CHAPTER 9

Weathering, Soil and Erosion

Discussion

We open Unit III, Surface Processes, with this chapter on weathering, soil, and erosion. These topics focus attention on the interactions among rocks, air, water, and life.

In addition to descriptions of mechanical weathering and chemical weathering, we emphasize that natural processes do not always fit into discrete categories, and we stress that mechanical and chemical weathering processes commonly work together and enhance each other.

Chemical weathering not only affects rocks, but also structures and industrial materials. Unpolluted moist air is corrosive by itself. Acid rain produced by air pollutants is even more corrosive and causes billions of dollars worth of damage each year. As a result of natural compounds and pollutants, steel buildings and bridges in the United States are weathering. About half a century after it was built, portions of the elevated West Side Highway in New York City rusted through and collapsed, sending vehicles plummeting onto the roadway below. In 1988, New York's Williamsburg bridge was closed due to corrosion by the salt that is spread on the roadway every winter.

Chapter 21 discusses the formation and availability of geological resources. Since there is often insufficient time to include this chapter at the end of a course, some instructors may chose to incorporate some of the topics into earlier chapters. If this strategy is chosen, you may wish to include "Weathering Processes that Form Ore Deposits", from Chapter 21 here.

Discussions of the nature of soil and the processes that form soils are integrated with descriptions of human use and abuse of soils.

Natural erosion and transport of sediment by streams, glaciers, and wind are the subjects of the following three chapters. In the last three sections of this chapter, we describe mass wasting: erosion by gravity. Mass wasting is a common natural event that frequently affects humans and their creations. The total average damage from landslides in one year equals that caused by earthquakes in 20 years. That fact stimulates students' interest in mass wasting.

Mass wasting accompanies many other geological processes, and creates many familiar landforms. We have already discussed landslides and debris flows initiated by earthquakes and volcanic eruptions in Chapters 6 and 7, respectively. Valleys widen as a result of stream or glacial erosion accompanied by mass wasting. Angular topography forms in deserts where vertically jointed cliffs collapse as a result of undercutting by streams, and mass wasting is common along sea coasts as waves undercut cliffs.

An obvious similarity exists between some landslides and avalanches. A powder avalanche is analogous to flow; the snow crystals move independently of one another. A slab avalanche is analogous to a slide because it occurs when consolidated chunks of snow break away and begin to move as coherent units. Hanging glaciers can fracture to release free-falling ice avalanches.

In both avalanches and mass wasting, it is relatively easy to identify areas of potential hazard, but often quite difficult to predict when failure will occur and motion will begin. Obviously a trigger such as heavy precipitation or an earthquake can initiate movement, but even with the best modeling, surprises occur.

Case studies are presented to illustrate mass wasting processes. They include descriptions of the Gros Ventre slide in Wyoming, the Madison River slide in Montana that killed 26 people sleeping in a campground, and mass wasting resulting from the 1980 Mount St. Helens eruption.

Three Focus On boxes provide additional material to supplement the text. Many geology students are non-majors and many instructors plan their courses for students with little or no background in mathematics or chemistry. However, for interested students, we provide "Representative Reactions in Chemical Weathering". "The Hubbard Brook Experimental Forest" and "Soil Erosion and Agriculture" introduce important environmental subjects, and again stress Earth systems interactions.

Answers to Discussion Questions

1. (a) mechanical; (b) chemical (oxidation); (c) chemical (dissolution); (d) chemical (precipitation); (e) exfoliation is frequently explained as a form of mechanical weathering, but if hydrolysis is important as discussed in the text, chemical weathering also contributes to exfoliation; (f) again, the distinction between mechanical and chemical weathering is not always entirely clear-cut. Frost wedging is clearly mechanical, but it occurs when water freezes, which is a chemical process.

2. If water contracted when it freezes, rocks would not be pushed apart and frost wedging would not occur. Thus mechanical weathering in cold climates would be greatly reduced.

3. In both processes, expansion occurs because crystal formation pushes rock apart. The main difference is that frost wedging is a phase change whereas salt cracking occurs as a result of chemical precipitation.

4. (a) Oxidation would be significant in the hot, dense, oxygen rich environment. On Earth, reactions between carbon dioxide and water vapor produce acids. Since no carbon dioxide exists

on Planet X, dissolution would be less pronounced unless other acid-forming compounds are present. The temperature never drops below the freezing point of water, so frost wedging would not occur. Root wedging and chemical weathering initiated by living organisms would not exist. Abrasion by wind-blown particles would occur. In this temperature range, water vapor would condense producing surface streams that would erode, transport, and deposit sediment. (b) The conditions outlined here are those found on Earth.

5. In the Arctic, summers are short and plant growth is slow. In addition, decay is so slow that little nutrient recycling and accumulation of humus occur. Therefore, soils are generally poor in the arctic. In the temperate regions, decay is relatively rapid in summer but slow in winter. This balance creates rich soils. Some of the plant litter decomposes and nutrients are recycled, but at the same time a reservoir of litter and nutrients is retained in the soil.

6. Mass wasting is uncommon on the Moon as evidenced by prominent 4 billion year old meteorite craters. As mentioned in the question, gravitation is weaker on the Moon than on the Earth. In addition, most mass wasting on Earth occurs after some other process de-stabilizes a slope. A stream or glacier may undermine a hillside, rainfall lubricates and adds weight to surface rock or regolith, earthquakes shake the surface, or volcanic eruptions melt large quantities of ice. These processes are nonexistent on the Moon.

7. In the chaparral of southern California and other areas with alternate dry and wet seasons, the vegetation is often destroyed by wildfires during the dry season. If heavy rain then falls on the barren ground during the wet season, there are no roots to hold the soil and absorb moisture, so mass wasting is likely.

A similar scenario also occurs in wetter environments. A recent study shows that much of the surface topography in the Yellowstone Park region formed after catastrophic fires similar to the 1988 fire.

8. (a) No mass wasting; (b) Very susceptible, especially if a stream flows at the base of the slope and undercuts it. Devegetation by wildfires would be a factor. (c) The slope is less susceptible if rocks dip away from the slope, or are horizontal, although mudflows and debris flows may occur; (d) again, very susceptible.

9. If this project is pursued, an additional exercise is to determine what types of building regulations (if any) apply to construction on potentially unstable slopes.

10. A mudflow killed 20,000 people in Armero, Columbia in 1985 when the volcano Nevado del Ruiz erupted nearly 50 kilometers away. The eruption itself occurred on an unpopulated

mountain, and hence, was not deadly, but the mudflow followed stream valleys to populated areas. Other examples of disastrous mass wasting caused by less damaging eruptions and earthquakes are cited in the text.

On the other hand, the earthquakes in San Francisco and Los Angeles in the early 1990s caused little mass wasting; most of the damage was from the quakes themselves.

11. The only foolproof solution is to remove all structures that lie down-valley from the major glaciers on Mount Baker. But this solution is impractical, people won't abandon their homes and businesses; they are willing, instead, to accept risk of mud slides initiated by a volcanic eruption. The only reasonable approach is to monitor the mountain for signs of an impending eruption. If an eruption seems imminent, then authorities can suggest or order an evacuation.

Mount St. Helens provided abundant warning that an eruption was about to occur. In addition, it lies in a rural area. Because the geologic evidence was strong and the economic loss from evacuation was low, it was relatively easy to make the decision order an evacuation. In Armero, geologists knew that the town lay in the path of a potential mudslide, but the volcano erupted without enough warning to warrant evacuation.

Looking into the future in the region around Mt Baker, no one can say what will happen. Authorities are committed to warning people of disaster, but are also reluctant to cause alarm or to order an expensive evacuation unless the danger signs are compelling.

Selected Reading

A general reference for all of Unit III is:
Michael A. Summerfield, *Global Geomorphology: An Introduction to the Study of Landforms.* New York: John Wiley and Sons, 1990. 537 pages.

An interesting article on weathering explains how desert arches form:
Ruth Flanagan, "Arches: A Tale of Desert and Sea." *Earth*, November 1994.

Several references on soil and soil fertility are:
Boyd G. Ellis and Henry D. Foth, *Soil Fertility, Second Edition.* Boca Raton, FL: Lewis Publishers, 1997, 304 pages.

Ray Miller and Ray Donahue, *Soils: An Introduction to Soils and Plant Growth.* Englewood Cliffs, NJ: Prentice-Hall, 1990. 752 pages.

Robert L. Wershaw, "Model for Humus in Soils and Sediments." *Environmental Science and*

Technology, 27(5), 1993.

We recommend four sources on soil erosion, agriculture, and food supply:
John Bongaarts, "Can the Growing Human Population Feed Itself?" *Scientific American*, March 1994.

Francesca Bray, "Agriculture for Developing Nations." *Scientific American*, July 1994.

Lester Brown et al., *State of the World 1995*. New York: Norton/Worldwatch, 1995;

David Pimentel et al., "Environmental and Economic Costs of Soil Erosion and Conservation Benefits." *Science, 267*, February 24, 1995.

Mass wasting is discussed in
Anders Rapp, Jian Li, and Rolf Nyberg "Mudflow Disasters in Mountainous Areas." *Ambio* 20, September 1991.

Chapter 9 Test

Multiple Choice:

1. Weathering is the decomposition and disintegration of rocks and minerals at the Earth's surface by
(a) mechanical processes only; (b) chemical processes only; (c) both mechanical and chemical processes; (d) internal processes.

2. Wind, flowing water, glaciers, and gravity are
(a) agents of erosion; (b) agents of isostasy; (c) agents of internal processes; (d) agents of orogeny.

3. In the weathering process of pressure release fracturing
(a) bedrock expands and fractures when the overlying rock erodes away; (b) bedrock minerals decompose to clay; (c) salts crystallize in cracks enlarging fractures; (d) bedrock dissolves and ground water carries the dissolved ions away.

4. During _____ water reacts with a mineral to form a new mineral with the water incorporated into its crystal structure.
(a) dissolution; (b) hydrolysis; (c) frost wedging; (d) salt cracking; (e) pressure-release fracturing.

5. Halite (common table salt) weathers in water by the process of
(a) dissolution; (b) hydrolysis; (c) frost wedging; (d) salt cracking; (e) pressure-release fracturing.

6. Atmospheric carbon dioxide dissolves in rainwater and reacts to form
(a) a weak acid; (b) a weak base; (c) a strong acid; (d) a strong base; (e) none of these.

7. During hydrolysis, feldspar weathers to form
(a) quartz; (b) sand; (c) gravel; (d) clay; (e) carbonic acid.

8. The least soluble major mineral in granite is
(a) quartz; (b) feldspar; (c) calcite; (d) mica.

9. _____ is a layer of loose rock fragments mixed with clay, silt, and sand overlying bedrock.
(a) Loam (b) Humus (c) Regolith or soil (d) Litter (e) Cap rock

10. Phosphorus, nitrogen, and potassium are examples of
(a) loam; (b) humus; (c) soil nutrients; (d) litter; (e) soil horizons.

11. The soil layer in which you would find the most organic material is the
(a) B horizon; (b) O horizon; (c) C horizon; (d) zone of leaching.

12. In soils, leached ions and clay frequently accumulate in the
(a) B horizon; (b) O horizon; (c) A horizon; (D) C horizon.

13. Tropical soils often contain high proportions of
(a) iron and sodium (b) iron and aluminum; (c) sodium and calcium; (d) aluminum and calcium.

14. Soil on a hillside is generally _____ than on the valley floor.
(a) deeper and richer (b) thinner and poorer (c) younger and richer (d) deeper and poorer

15. Soil is usually only a _____ thick or less in most parts of the world.
(a) hundred meters (b) few meters (c) few centimeters (d) few kilometers

16. The _____ is the maximum slope or steepness at which loose material remains stable.
(a) angle of repose (b) mass wasting angle (c) dip slope (d) slip slope

17. During _____, loose, unconsolidated regolith moves downslope as a viscous fluid.
(a) slide (b) fall (c) flow (d) slump

18. Typically, soil creep occurs at a rate of
(a) about 1 centimeter per year; (b) about 1 meter per year; (c) about 20 centimeters per year; (d) about 1 kilometer per year.

19. The type of mass wasting known as slump occurs when
(a) fine grained particles flow downslope; (b) rock and soil fall freely down the face of a steep cliff; (c) water-saturated soil slides over permafrost; (d) blocks of material slide downhill over curved fractures

20.The landslide that occurred in Kelly, Wyoming is an example of a/an
(a) rockslide, or rock avalanche; (b) slump; (c) slip; (d) fall.

21. The mass wasting that created devastation near the Madison River in Montana was triggered by
(a) improper irrigation; (b) an earthquake; (c) a volcano; (d) heavy rain and snow melt.

22. A defense against mass-wasting damage on a hillside is
(a) to study an area's geology to determine if landslides have occurred on similar nearby slopes; (b) to saturate the slope with water; (c) to bulldoze away lower parts of the slope; (d) to clear away all the trees and shrubs on upper parts of the hill.

True or False:

1. Erosion is the decomposition and disintegration of rocks and minerals at the Earth's surface.

2. Weathering involves little or no movement of the decomposed rocks and minerals.

3. Hydrolysis is an example of mechanical weathering.

4. Oxidation in rocks occurs when iron in minerals reacts with oxygen.

5. During hydrolysis, moving water carries off most of the aluminum originally present in feldspar.

6. If you live in a moist climate, would be likely to find halite in your backyard.

7. Acidic and basic solutions have greater abilities to dissolve rocks and minerals than does pure water.

8. When acidic rainwater seeps into cracks in limestone, it dissolves the rock, enlarging the cracks to form caves and caverns.

9. The alternate shrinking and swelling of humus keeps soil loose, allowing roots to grow easily.

10. Biological, geologic, and chemical processes all affect nutrient transport.

11. The total global property damage from landslides in a single year equals that caused by earthquakes in 20 years.

12. If rock layers dip at an angle perpendicular to the slope of the hillside, the slope may be stable even if it is undercut.

13. Talus can maintain an angle of repose up to 45°.

14. Added water seldom triggers landslides.

15. Landslides are common in desert environments.

16. Volcanic activity may initiate slides by melting snow and ice near the tops of volcanoes.

17. Fall is the slowest type of mass wasting.

18. Excessive irrigation can trigger slump.

19. You can distinguish slump from creep by the orientations of the trees.

Completion:

1. Decomposition and disintegration of rocks and minerals at the surface by mechanical and chemical processes is _____.

2. The removal of weathered material is _____.

3. The physical disintegration of rocks is _____ _____.

4. The mechanical wearing and grinding of rock surfaces by friction and impact is called _____.

5. Alteration of the composition of rocks and minerals by the interaction of air and water at the Earth's surface is _____ _____.

6. Rusting is a form of _____.

7. If the hydroxyl ion (OH^-) concentration in a water solution is greater than the hydrogen ion (H^+) concentration, the solution is a _____.

8. The process whereby salts precipitate and grow in cracks or between mineral grains in a rock, thereby pushing them apart is called _____ _____.

9. As feldspar weathers to clay, water reacts with the feldspar in a process called _____.

10. The most fertile type of soil, called _____, is composed of a mixture of sand, clay, silt, and generous amounts of organic matter.

11. The B soil horizon is also called the zone of _____.

12. In a dry climate, dissolved ions may precipitate in the B horizon, forming a _____.

13. Tropical rainforest soils, called _____ soils, contain only the most insoluble cations.

14. _____ is a hard cement that forms when calcium carbonate precipitates in soil.

15. A highly aluminous soil called _____ is the world's main source of aluminum ore.

16. _____ consists of chunks of rock that break off from cliffs, fall, and collect downslope.

17. During _____, loose, unconsolidated regolith moves as a fluid.

18. Slow downhill movement of rock or soil under the influence of gravity is _____.

19. A flowing mixture of clay, silt, sand, and rock in which more than half of the particles are larger than sand is called a/an _____ _____.

20. A layer of permanently frozen soil or subsoil is called _____.

21. A/an _____ occurs when blocks of rock or soil slide downslope over a gently curved fracture.

22. _____ is the rapid movement of a newly detached segment of bedrock.

23. _____ provide level surfaces to reduce both mass wasting and erosion, and also form stable platforms for vegetation.

Answers for Chapter 9

Multiple Choice: 1. c; 2. a; 3. a; 4. b; 5. a; 6. a; 7. d; 8. a; 9. c; 10. c; 11. b; 12. a; 13. b; 14. b; 15. b; 16. a; 17. c; 18. a; 19. d; 20. a; 21. b; 22. a

True or False: 1. F; 2. T; 3. F; 4. T; 5. F; 6. F; 7. T; 8. T; 9. T; 10. T; 11. T; 12. T; 13. T; 14. F; 15. T; 16. T; 17. F; 18. T; 19. T.

Completion: 1. weathering; 2. erosion; 3. mechanical weathering; 4. abrasion; 5. chemical weathering; 6. oxidation or chemical weathering; 7. base; 8. salt cracking; 9. hydrolysis; 10. loam; 11. accumulation; 12. pedocal, or caliche zone; 13. laterite; 14. Caliche; 15. bauxite; 16. Talus; 17. flow; 18. creep; 19. debris flow; 20. permafrost; 21. slump; 22. Fall; 23. Terraces

CHAPTER 10

Fresh Water: Streams, Lakes, Ground Water, and Wetlands

Discussion

Chapter 10 describes and discusses fresh water - perhaps the single most valuable geologic resource, and the most important agent in the Earth's surface processes. Only 0.64 percent of the Earth's water is non-salty and accessible to humans. The remaining 99.36 percent is sea water and glacial ice. The accessible fresh water resides in streams, lakes, ground water reservoirs, and wetlands. The chapter begins with a description of the hydrologic cycle - the processes by which water continuously recycles among land, sea, and the atmosphere.

Many geological processes occur simultaneously. However, a teacher or book can only teach one concept at a time. In many cases, problems arising from this dilemma are easily resolved and a logical pedagogic order reveals itself. However, in discussing streams it seems that everything must be taught first. A stream doesn't first erode sediment, then transport it, and finally deposit it. Rather all three processes may occur at the same time in almost the same location. Similarly, changes in channel shape, sediment load, discharge, velocity, and tectonic rejuvenation are so closely interrelated that it becomes misleading to separate the topics into discrete sections. There is no choice but to teach one topic at a time, but it is also important to remind the student that nature is not always as sequential as a textbook. The instructor might introduce placer deposits from Chapter 21, in the discussion of deposition in stream beds.

Flooding, one of the most common and costly of all geologic hazards, is discussed in this section. We use the 1993 Mississippi River food as a springboard to discuss flood control and flood plain management.

Lakes are some of the Earth's most fragile and ephemeral landforms. We stress that modern humans live in a special time in Earth history when the Earth's surface is dotted with numerous lakes primarily because glacial ice, which created millions of lake and pond basins, has disappeared from much of the Earth's surface only within the past 12,000 to 18,000 years. We then discuss the formation, evolution, and ultimate destruction of lakes as a result of their natural development.

Sections 10.6 and 10.7 describe ground water, its movement, and human use of ground water. We stress that 60 times more fresh water is stored in subterranean aquifers than in all surface water combined, and that about half of the people in the United States rely on ground water for drinking.

We then describe the role of ground water in development of karst, geysers, and geothermal energy resources. Finally, a section on wetlands emphasizes their varied nature and their importance as ecosystems for wildlife support and as natural water purification systems.

We return to the subject of water resources in Chapter 20, Water Pollution.

Answers to Discussion Questions

1. (a) If global temperature rose, more water would evaporate from the oceans and therefore precipitation and runoff on the continents would increase. Climatologists also calculate that global warming might lead to changes in wind and current patterns. Monsoon cycles in Asia and jet streams in higher latitudes might be altered. If so, rainfall patterns would change, humid areas might be desertified, deserts could receive more rainfall. These changes could affect agriculture and the economy in many areas. A rise in temperature might also lead to melting of the Greenland and Antarctic ice caps and a rise in sea level, although this scenario is uncertain. The effect of melting of coastal glaciers could be offset if increased precipitation led to an increase in the amount of permanent ice on continents. The situation is further complicated by the fact that the climate in some areas in Northern Canada and the USSR is cold enough for glaciation if more moisture were available. Therefore, paradoxically, a warming trend could initiate glaciation in some places. This topic is discussed further in Chapter 18, Climate Change.

(b) If global temperature fell, less water would evaporate from the oceans and therefore precipitation and runoff on the continents would decrease. Semiarid lands could be desertified. Again patterns of precipitation might change, with unknown consequences. Ice would be retained longer and in some areas glaciers would expand.

2. If the stream is constricted, the water behind the constriction would be partially blocked and would slow down. Upstream, sediment might accumulate as the current slowed. In contrast, velocity at the constriction would increase. This increase in velocity would increase downstream erosion. The channel would deepen or widen, or both, downstream.

3. The effects of artificial levees and some other types of flood control structures are discussed in the section on the 1993 Mississippi River flood. The bottom line is that human attempts to control floods can have beneficial effects sometimes and locally, but commonly create long-term negative effects and increase damage away from the locality of the flood control structures.

4. Two types of benefits may result from NFIP. The program insures people who live in flood plains when a flood destroys their homes, so that they do not lose everything they own. In addition, new structures must be built to resist flood damage. The major negative effect of NFIP is that people who own structures that sustain less than 50 percent damage can use taxpayers'

dollars to rebuild structures that are likely to be damaged again in the following flood. Thus, homeowners can ignore an obvious geological hazard at taxpayers expense.

5. The fact that a 100-year flood occurred recently is irrelevant. A 100-year flood has a 1 percent probability of occurring in any year, and thus, a 50 percent probability in 50 years. You must decide if a 50 percent probability of flood damage over 50 years is balanced by the economic and other benefits of siting a business on the flood plain. Most state and local laws prohibit new construction on the most vulnerable sites.

6. During the summer, the lake in our imaginary world would be identical to a lake in the real world, with warm water on the top and cold water below the thermocline. During the fall, the surface water in the imaginary lake would cool, become denser, and settle, causing a fall turnover, just as in the real lake. The difference would start when the temperature dropped below 4°C. In the real world, cold water below 4°C floats on the deeper water which is a little warmer than 4°C. In the imaginary world, the cold water below 4°C would sink, and when surface water froze, the ice would sink. Thus, in winter in the imaginary world, ice would collect on the bottom of the lake. Mid sized lakes in temperate regions would freeze solid and aquatic ecosystems as we know them couldn't exist. In spring surface water would warm, there would be no spring turnover. It is uncertain what would happen to the ice on the bottom of the lake. Depending on the depth and latitude, ice might remain on the bottom all year round, or it might melt due to conduction of heat through water, soil, or rock. Because there would be no spring turnover the deeper water would be less oxygenated than it is in lakes in the real world.

7. This type of failure is common and could occur if the well were dug into impermeable rock or regolith such as unfractured granite, clay, or shale.

8. In a desert, the water table commonly lies below a stream bed. Consequently, water seeps from the stream bed into the ground and eventually downward to the water table. In wetter environments the surface of a stream or lake lies at the lowest points of land, in valley bottoms. The water table generally rises and falls with the land surface, and ground water flows from places where the water table is highest toward places where it is lowest. As a result, ground water flows toward the lowest points of land - those occupied by streams and lakes - and feeds the streams and lakes.

9. Karst landscapes are generally found in limestone terrain because limestone is a common highly soluble rock. Some karst landscapes occur in regions where sedimentary gypsum deposits, which are also very soluble, lie near the surface.

10. Wetlands support large and diverse wildlife populations for several reasons. Wetlands water is normally very rich in nutrients, which results in lush plant growth. The abundance of water also supports a rich vegetative cover. Wetlands provide excellent cover from predators as well as food for wildlife. Wetlands also offer shallow-water environments necessary for breeding, spawning, and other reproductive activities necessary for many kinds of wildlife. In ecology, boundaries between ecosystems, called ecotones, often support greater numbers of organisms and species than either adjoining ecosystem. Thus, the brush along fence lines between forests and fields supports more species of birds than either the forest or the field. One reason for this increase in species is that an organism in the ecotone can exploit niches in either system or it can exploit the specialized niches in the ecotone. Wetlands - the boundary between land and water -- provides benefits of both land and water and the combination provides more habitats and growth than either system by itself.

11. The shallow, nutrient-rich, and often warm waters of wetlands support great populations of plants and microbial decomposer organisms. The plants extract dissolved nutrients from the water, thereby purifying it. The decomposers consume sewage and other solid and semi-solid organic material, converting it to water, carbon dioxide, and dissolved nutrients, which are then consumed by plants.

12. Until the mid-1960s, most Americans considered wetlands to be mosquito-infested, malarial swamps occupying land that could be farmed or otherwise developed if drained or filled. Recently, however, Americans have realized that wetlands naturally cleanse polluted water and regulate water flow to reduce drought during dry times and floods during wet times. Wetlands also provide habitat for wildlife, are the breeding grounds for many food fish and other kinds of animals, and offer recreational resources to hunters, wildlife watchers, and boaters. As a result, environmental and recreational organizations have become politically active on behalf of wetlands preservation. The political activity has decreased the rate at which wetlands are being lost from the country.

Selected Reading

Many excellent, recently written, books and articles about streams and surface water are available, including the following:

Peter H. Gleick, ed., *Water in Crisis, A Guide to the World's Fresh Water Resources*. Oxford: Oxford Science Publications, 1993, 473 pages.

C.T. Haan, B.J. Barfield, and J.C. Hayes, *Design Hydrology and Sedimentology for Small Catchments*. San Diego: Academic Press, 1994, 681 pages.

Luna Leopold, *A View of the River*. Boston: Harvard University Press, 1994.

Malcolm Newson, *Hydrology and the River Environment*. Cambridge: MIT Press, 1994.

Alice Outwater, *Water: A Natural History*. New York: Basic Books, 1996, 210 pages.

Tim Palmer, *Lifelines, The Case for River Conservation*. Washington, DC: Island Press, 1994.

Sandra Postel, *The Last Oasis*, New York: Norton, 1992.

A provocative article on flood control is found in:
Nancy Philippi, "Plugging the Gaps in Flood-Control Policy." *Issues in Science and Technology*, Winter 1994-95 p. 73-78.

General reference resources on ground water are:
Mary P. Anderson and William W. Woesssner, *Applied Groundwater Modeling*. San Diego: Academic Press, 1992, 381 pages.

Janine Gilbert, Dan L. Danielpool, and Jack Stanfoprd, eds., *Groundwater Ecology*. Orlando: Academic, 1994, 571 pages.

John E. Moore, Alexander Zaporozec, and James W. Mercer, *Groundwater--A Primer*. Annapolis, Md.: American Geological Institute, 1995.

Herbert F. Wang and Mary P. Anderson, *Introduction to Groundwater Modeling*. New York: Academic Press, 1995, 237 pages.

Wetlands are discussed in:
Patrick Dugan, ed., *Wetlands in Danger: A World Conservation Atlas*. New York: Oxford University Press, 1993, 187 pages.

Mary E. Kentual et al., *Wetlands, An Approach to Improving Decision Making in Wetland Restoration and Creation*. Washington D.C.: Island Press, 1992.

Jon A. Kusler and Mary E. Kentual, eds., *Wetland Creation and Restoration*. Washington D.C.:

92

Island Press, 1990, 594 pages.

George Mulamootitil, Barry G. Warner, and Edward A. McBean, eds., *Wetlands: Environmental Gradients, Boundaries, and Buffers*. Boca Raton, FL: Lewis Publishers, 1996, 320 pages.

World Wildlife Fund, *Statewide Wetland Strategies*. Washington D.C.: Island Press, 1992.

Chapter 10 Test

Multiple Choice:

1. What proportion of the Earth's surface water is fresh water found in streams, lakes, wetlands,and ground-water reservoirs?
(a) less than 1 percent; (b) 5 percent; (c) 25 percent; (d) 50 percent.

2. What proportion of the Earth's surface water is salty sea water?
(a) less than 5 percent; (b) 25 percent; (c) 75 percent; (d) more than 95 percent.

3. What proportion of the Earth's surface water is frozen in glaciers?
(a) less than 0.1 percent; (b) 1.8 percent; (c) 11.3 percent; (d) more than 95 percent.

4. Stream gradient, discharge, and channel shape determine the _____ of a stream.
(a) age; (b) color; (c) velocity; (d) salinity.

5. A stream's discharge is
(a) greatest during a time of low water; (b) greatest during a flood; (c) minimal during a flood; (d) constant regardless of water level.

6. A stream's capacity is
(a) greatest during a time of low water; (b) greatest during a flood; (c) minimal during a flood; (d) constant regardless of water level.

7. A stream's competence is
(a) greatest during a time of low water; (b) greatest during a flood; (c) minimal during a flood; (d) constant regardless of water level.

8. Streams round rock and sediment directly by
(a) abrasion; (b) solution; (c) hydraulic action; (d) competence; (e) none of these.

9. The ions carried in solution in a stream constitute the
(a) abrasion load; (b) suspended load; (c) bed load; (d) dissolved load; (e) saltation factor.

10. Most sediment is carried in most streams by
(a) saltation (b) traction (c) solution (d) suspension (e) abrasion

11. The water on the outside of a stream curve moves
(a) faster than the water on the inside; (b) slower than the water on the inside; (c) the same speed as the water on the inside; (d) mostly vertically in a process called upwelling.

12. When a stream has a greater supply of sediment than it can carry,
(a) it forms a braided stream; (b) it cuts a single channel; (c) it stops overflowing its banks; (d) it stops flowing.

13. The ultimate base level of most streams is
(a) the low-water benchmark; (b) flood stage; (c) natural levee; (d) sea level; (e) elevation of the confluence.

14. The top of a waterfall is an example of
(a) ultimate base level; (b) temporary or local base level; (c) the low-water benchmark; (d) a natural levee; (e) none of these.

15. Low-gradient streams are likely to form
(a) V shaped valleys; (b) U shaped valleys; (c) numerous waterfalls; (d) valleys with meanders and oxbow lakes in their flood plains; (e) steep gullies.

16. The region ultimately drained by a single river is a
(a) flood plain; (b) channel; (c) drainage divide; (d) drainage basin; (e) base level

17. The portion of a valley covered by water during a flood is the
(a) natural levee; (b) delta; (c) flood plain; (d) meander.

18. A kettle lake formed when
(a) melting glaciers left huge blocks of ice in glacial sediment; (b) advancing glaciers scoured bedrock; (c) a fault opened a deep rift in the crust; (d) a stream scoured a temporary base level.

19. An oligotrophic lake
(a) has a high nutrient supply; (b) is generally shallow enough so sunlight reaches the bottom; (c) forms when sewage and phosphate detergents flow into a lake; (d) has a low productivity.

20. Ground water
(a) is easy to clean up once it is polluted; (b) is an infinite resource; (c) seeps upward into desert streams; (d) provides drinking water for more than half the population of North America.

21. Sedimentary rocks are
(a) generally less porous than igneous rocks; (b) generally more porous than igneous rocks; (c) equally porous as igneous rocks; (d) less likely to contain ground water than igneous rocks.

22. Clay has
(a) high porosity and high permeability; (b) high porosity and low permeability; (c) low porosity and low permeability; (d) low porosity and high permeability.

23. The region of the crust in which all pore spaces contain water is
(a) asthenosphere; (b) zone of accumulation; (c) zone of ablation; (d) zone of saturation; (e) zone of aeration.

24. An aquifer is
(a) both porous and permeable; (b) porous but not permeable; (c) usually found in unfractured igneous and metamorphic rock; (d) permeable but not porous.

25. In a typical aquifer, ground water flows at
(a) the rate of surface rivers; (b) about 4 meters per day; (c) about 15 meters per year; (d) 1 to 2 cm per year; (e) twice the rate of surface runoff.

26. In a desert
(a) streams feed ground water reserves; (b) ground water feeds streams; (c) the water table lies above stream beds; (d) there is no ground water.

27. Springs develop
(a) where the water table intersects the land surface; (b) in the unsaturated zone; (c) underground; (d) only in deserts.

28. Water in an artesian aquifer rises without being pumped because
(a) water in the lower part of the aquifer is under pressure from the weight of rock above; (b) water in the upper part of the aquifer is under pressure from the weight of water below; (c) the rock is not permeable; (d) it is an inclined aquifer bounded by impermeable rock;

29. Caverns usually form in
(a) granite; (b) limestone; (c) fractured schist; (d) conglomerate; (e) shale

30. In the past century, the United States has lost more than _____ of its wetlands to agriculture and development.

(a) 25 percent (b) 10 percent (c) 50 percent (d) 95 percent

True or False:

1. The velocity of a stream increases when discharge increases.

2. Water flows more rapidly near the banks than near the center of a stream.

3. Clay and silt are small enough that even the slight turbulence of a slow stream keeps them in suspension.

4. When stream current slows down, the stream loses its ability to transport the largest particles and deposits them in the stream bed.

5. A stream erodes its bank most rapidly on the inside of a curve.

6. Braided streams are rare in both deserts and glacial environments.

7. A graded stream has little net erosion or deposition.

8. Streams never flow through mountains, ridges, or high plateaus.

9. A rapidly flowing stream can carry sand in suspension.

10. Deltas are permanent unchanging geologic features.

11. As a stream rises to flood stage, its discharge increases but its velocity decreases.

12. A 100-year flood happens regularly every 100 years.

13. The fine sediment carried in flood water accumulates on flood plains to form fertile soils.

14. A steep mountain stream usually cuts a U-shaped valley.

15. A eutrophic lake is likely to support abundant vegetation and may be covered by a mat of rooted and floating plants.

16. If you dig into the unsaturated zone, the hole will fill with water.

17. The water table rises and falls with the seasons.

18. Groundwater exists in moist environments, but not in arid or semiarid environments.

19. Subsidence is a readily reversible process.

20. A wetland is wet all the time.

21. One third of all endangered species of both plants and animals in the United States depend on wetlands for survival.

Completion:

1. The constant circulation of water among sea, land, and the atmosphere is called the _____ _____.

2. The _____ of a stream is a measure of the largest particle it can carry.

3. The _____ of a stream is the total amount of sediment it can carry past a point in a given amount of time.

4. _____ is a mode of transport in which water turbulence keeps fine particles mixed with the water and prevents them from settling to the bottom.

5. If stream velocity is sufficient, sand grains bounce along in a series of short leaps or hops called _____.

6. A/an _____ is an elongate mound of sediment in a stream channel.

7. A/an _____ _____ is a gently sloping mound of sediment deposited where a stream issues from a narrow canyon onto a plain or valley floor.

8. When a stream enters a lake or the ocean, it deposits sediment to create a/an _____.

9. If a stream cuts through the narrow neck of land separating two meanders, the abandoned

meander loops may become isolated to form a/an _____ _____.

10. Downward stream erosion is called _____.

11. Sediment ridges on the margins of stream channels are called _____ _____.

12. During a flood, a stream overflows its banks and water covers the adjacent _____ _____.

13. _____ is the proportional volume of rock or soil that consists of open spaces.

14. _____ is a measure of the speed at which water can travel through porous soil or bedrock.

15. The_____ _____ is the top of the zone of saturation.

16. A/an _____ is any body of rock or soil that can yield economically significant quantities of water.

17. A desert stream, where water seeps from the stream bed to the ground water is called a/an _____ or _____ stream.

18. The top of a saturated zone created by an impermeable layer that lies above the main water table is called a/an _____ _____ _____.

19. Mineral deposits formed in caves by the action of water are called _____.

20. _____ hang from the ceiling of a cavern.

21. A/an _____ forms when the roof of a limestone cavern collapses.

22. A/an _____ erupts hot water and steam onto the Earth's surface.

23. Hot springs have been tapped to produce _____ _____.

24. Flood plains, marshes, and swamps are all _____.

Answers for Chapter 10

Multiple Choice: 1. a; 2. d; 3. b; 4. c; 5. b; 6. b; b. d; 8. a; 9. d; 10. d; 11. a; 12. a; 13. d; 14. b; 15. d; 16. d; 17. c; 18. a; 19. d; 20. d; 21. b; 22. b; 23. d; 24. a; 25. c; 26. a; 27. a; 28. d; 29. b; 30. c.

True or False: 1. T; 2. F; 3. T; 4. T; 5. F; 6. F; 7. T; 8. F; 9. T; 10. F; 11. F; 12. F; 13. T; 14. F; 15. T; 16. F; 17. T; 18. F; 19. F; 20. F; 21. T.

Completion: 1. hydrologic cycle; 2. competence; 3. capacity; 4. Suspension; 5. saltation; 6. bar; 7. alluvial fan; 8. delta; 9. oxbow lake; 10. downcutting; 11. natural levees; 12. flood plain; 13. Porosity; 14. Permeability; 15. water table; 16. aquifer; 17. influent, losing; 18. perched water table; 19. speleothems; 20. Stalactites; 21. sinkhole; 22. geyser; 23. geothermal energy; 24. wetlands

CHAPTER 11

Glaciers and Ice Ages

Discussion

During our discussion of glacial movement, we return to two concepts introduced in previous chapters on rocks and plate tectonics: phase changes initiated by changes in pressure and plastic behavior of solids. In Chapter 5, we explained that hot mantle rock melts when pressure is reduced. In this chapter we explain that an increase in pressure melts ice. There is no contradiction here, the difference arises because rock expands as it melts, whereas ice contracts as it melts. As a demonstration, suspend an ice cube in a freezer and hang a thin wire over it. Then weight the wire on both ends and leave it for a week. The ice directly under the wire melts, due to the pressure. The meltwater refreezes above the wire as soon as the pressure is removed. Eventually the wire migrates entirely through the ice cube but does not cut it in half.

It is more difficult to illustrate the plastic behavior of snow and ice, especially for students who live in warm climates. However, if you live in an area with abundant snowfall, you need only tell students to observe snow curling as it slowly creeps off a roof to convince them of the plasticity of ice.

Most of the chapter focuses on the formation and movement of a glacier. In turn, glacial movement causes erosion, transport, and deposition.

The section on the Milankovitch could easily be moved to Chapter 18 on climate change. However, this material is customarily taught in the discussion of glaciers, so we include it here. This is a good time to reinforce the concept that the two million year time span of Pleistocene glaciation is really a thin slice of geologic time. The first tool-making human ancestors evolved roughly two million years ago. Case Studies on, "Pleistocene Glaciers and the Great Lakes" and "Glacial Lake Missoula and the Greatest Flood in North America" emphasize the tremendous effect of the most recent Ice Sheet.

Answers to Discussion Questions

1. A glacier flows more slowly than a stream. Although a glacier moves partly by plastic flow, it is solid. There is no turbulence analogous to that of stream flow. Glaciers are more viscous and transport much larger particles. They can also be considerably larger and more massive than a river; they fill entire valleys rather than a narrow channel, and erode valley walls as well as floors, forming U-shaped valleys.

2. (a) The glacier would retreat; (b) The glacier would advance; (c) The glacier would advance, especially if the summer temperature decreased.

3. Plastic flow is only significant for ice buried 40 to 50 meters beneath the surface. Small thin alpine glaciers in many portions of the Rocky Mountains and elsewhere contain mostly rigid ice and only a thin layer of plastic ice. In contrast, on the much thicker continental glaciers of Greenland and Antarctica, the brittle layer is a thin surface veneer and nearly all the ice is plastic.

4. Not enough snow falls in winter, so all the snow melts even though the summers are relatively short and cool.

5. Compare the rock type of the boulder with that of the country rock, look for other evidence of glaciation, such glacial till or striations on the boulders or on bedrock. Search in the direction that a glacier came from for country rock similar to that of the boulder.

6. We wrote this question to reinforce the concept that a glacier moves even though its terminus may remain stationary or even retreat. Thus the ice in any cross section of a glacier moves downslope, but the entire glacier does not. Geology authors try to relate geological concepts to convenient analogies, but analogies are usually only approximations of reality. Glaciers have been compared to both bulldozers and conveyor belts. While both comparisons are helpful, neither provides a completely accurate picture of glacial movement.

7. Moraines are typically unsorted and unstratified, stream sediment is typically sorted and layered. Sometimes the spaces between stream cobbles fill with sediment. However, if this occurs, the cobbles will still be in contact with one another. In a ground moraine, cobbles are commonly do not touch, but are suspended in a finer matrix. Angular cobbles and boulders are often deposited by a glacier. However, glaciers often transport and deposit sediment that was previously rounded during stream transport. Look for morainal landforms.

8. Medial moraines form when glaciers merge, and they can merge only if they are moving.

9. If you dug below the soil, a moraine would be composed of unsorted, unstratified sediment, easily distinguished from bedrock. The sediment would also be different from sediment deposited by a stream as explained in the answer to question 7, above.

Selected Reading

Two general references on glaciers are:
Douglas I. Benn, *Glaciers and Glaciation.* New York: John Wiley and Sons, 1997, 736 pages.

Michael Hambrey and Jurg Alean, *Glaciers*. New York: Cambridge University Press, 1994, 208 pages.

Detailed studies of glacial movement are given in:
Hermann Engelhardt, Neil Humphrey, Barclay Kamb, and Mark Fahnestock, "Physical Conditions at the Base of a Fast Moving Antarctic Ice Stream." *Science,248*(57) 1990.

R. Keith Raney, "Probing Ice Sheets with Imaging Radar." *Science, 262,* December 1993.

Glacial cycles are discussed in:
Wallace S. Broecker and George H. Denton, "What Drives Glacial Cycles?" *Scientific American,* January 1990.

Jon Erickson, *Ice Ages: Past and Future.* Summit, PA: Tab Books, 1991, 180 pages.

Kurt Lambeck and Masao Nakada, "Constraints on the Age and Duration of the Last Interglacial Period and on Sea-level Variation." *Nature, 357*, May 14, 1992.

A classic review of the Milankovitch theory is given in
J. D. Hays, John Imbrie, and N. J. Shackleton, "Variation in the Earth's Orbit: Pacemaker of the Ice Ages." *Science, 194*, December 1976.

Chapter 11 Test

Multiple Choice:

1. If snow survives through one summer, it converts to rounded ice grains called
(a) basal ice; (b) glacial ice; (c) firn; (d) ablation ice.

2. Glaciers form
(a) only near the equator; (b) on the surface of the Arctic ocean; (c) only on high mountain tops;
(d) near the equator, on high mountain tops, and near sea level; (e) only at high latitudes.

3. The ice sheets of Greenland and Antarctica contain ___ percent of the world's ice.
(a) 100 (b) 99 (c) 75 (d) 50 (e) 25

4. The Cordillera Darwin in southern Chile is a relatively warm and very wet mountain range.
The peaks rise steeply from the ocean. Which of the following statements about the glaciers in
this mountain range is correct?
(a) The primary mechanism of glacial movement is the oozing of ice under the great weight of the
central portion of the glaciers. (b) Because the ice is warm and plastic, there are relatively few
crevasses in the glaciers. (c) The ice slides so quickly downslope that it does not have time to
exhibit plastic behavior. (d) glacial movement is relatively fast as compared with glaciers in colder
drier continental ranges.

5. Near the base of a glacier the ice is
(a) extremely cold and brittle; (b) relatively warm and brittle; (c) fractured into crevasses; (d)
relatively plastic and often warm enough so that free water may flow along bedrock.

6. The higher elevation portion of a glacier where more snow accumulates in winter than melts in
summer is called
(a) the zone of accumulation; (b) the ablation area; (c) the zone of aeration; (d) snow line.

7. Imagine that over the past century the local temperature in a mountain range has become slightly cooler, yet the glaciers are receding. Which of the following explanations is most probable?
(a) As the air cooled, the glacier stopped moving and the lower elevations melted. (b) As the air cooled, less precipitation fell, bringing less winter snow. (c) Cooling made the ice more brittle so the glacier broke apart more easily. (d) Cooling made the ice more plastic, allowing it to flow faster to lowland elevations where it melted.

8. Imagine that a long-lasting glacier melted and a stream replaced the ice in the valley floor. After many years the valley shape could be best described as a
(a) deep U-shaped valley; (b) a deep V-shaped valley; (c) a valley that looks like a V cut into the bottom of a U; (d) a valley that looks like a U cut into the bottom of a V.

9. A sharp narrow ridge between glacial valleys is a/an
(a) bergshrund; (b) cirque; (c) horn; (d) arete; (e) drumlin.

10. When a glacier is at its greatest advance, it deposits a/an
(a) medial moraine; (b) terminal moraine; (c) recessional moraine; (d) ground moraine.

11. During an Ice Age,
(a) all the continental land is covered by a giant continental glacier; (b) the ice may advance and recede several times in response to alternate warm and dry times; (c) the high latitudes are ice covered but there are no glaciers near the equator; (d) glaciers extend into the sea and cover large portions of the oceans; (e) a and d.

12. When glaciers grow, global sea level
(a) falls; (b) rises; (c) remains constant.

True or False:

1. A glacier forms wherever the amount of snow that falls in winter exceeds the amount that melts in summer.

2. Rates of glacial movement depend entirely on slope steepness.

3. Pressure near the base of a glacier may cause ice at the base of a glacier to melt.

4. Ice near the base of a glacier fractures to form crevasses.

5. Frost wedging releases rocks from the cirque walls.

6. Glaciers form V-shaped valleys.

7. Extensive glacial deposits found in some places were carried by icebergs during catastrophic floods.

8. Ice is so much more viscous than water that it carries particles of all sizes together.

9. Sediment particles carried by a glacier are likely to be rounded by the erosive power of the ice.

10. Terminal moraines record the extent of continental glaciers of the most recent ice age.

11. Geologic evidence shows that the Earth has been cold and ice covered for about 90 percent of the past 2.5 billion years.

12. Much of the northern Great Plains, which form the fertile soil of the "breadbasket" of North America is covered with ground moraine, loess, or outwash.

Completion:

1. A/an _____ is a massive, long-lasting accumulation of compacted snow and ice that forms on land.

2. A glacier that covers an area of 50,000 square kilometers or more is a/an _____ _____.

3. The entire glacier slides over bedrock by _____ _____ like a bar of soap on a tilted board.

4. _____ form in the upper 50 meters of a glacier as it flows over bedrock.

5. A/an _____ is a lake that forms in a depression eroded into the base of a cirque.

6. A string of lakes, commonly connected by rapids and waterfalls, extending down valley from a glacial cirque is called _____ _____.

7. A/an _____ is a steep-walled semicircular depression eroded into mountain by a glacier.

8. A small glacial valley lying high above the floor of the main valley is called a/an _____ _____.

9. _____ _____ is sediment that was first carried by a glacier and then transported and deposited by a stream.

10. A mound of sediment in the center of an alpine glacier that is formed when two smaller glaciers merge is called a _____ _____.

11. A/an _____ is an long sinuous ridge that forms as the channel deposit of a stream that flowed within or beneath a melting glacier.

12. Glacial streams deposit their sediment downstream from the glacier as _____.

13. A time of extensive glacial growth, when alpine glaciers descend into lowland valleys and continental glaciers spread over higher latitudes, is called a/an _____ _____.

14. _____ occurs when the Earth's axis circles like a wobbling top.

Answers for Chapter 11

Multiple Choice: 1. c; 2. d; 3. b; 4. d; 5. d; 6. a; 7. b; 8. c; 9. d; 10. b; 11. b; 12. a

True or False: 1. T; 2. F; 3. T; 4. F; 5. T; 6. F; 7. F; 8. T; 9. F; 10. T; 11. F; 12. T

Completion: 1. glacier; 2. continental glacier; 3. basal slip; 4. Crevasses; 5. tarn; 6. paternoster lakes; 7. cirque; 8. hanging valley; 9. Stratified drift; 10. medial moraine 11. esker; 12. outwash; 13. ice age; 14. Precession

CHAPTER 12

Deserts and Wind

Discussion

Chapter 12 opens with a brief overview of the meteorological conditions that form deserts, followed by a discussion of typical desert landforms. Commercial evaporite deposits, Section 21.2, may be incorporated here with the material on playas. We emphasize that the world's deserts differ from one another in rock type, availability of sediment, topography, average temperature, and the dominant plant species; they are similar to one another only in that they all receive scant rainfall. In Section 12.3, we provide a brief overview of two desert landscapes in the United States. Although many differences exist between the Colorado Plateau and Death Valley, one of the most important is that the Colorado Plateau is drained by free-flowing streams, whereas Death Valley is not. Partially as a result of this difference, the Colorado Plateau is cut by deep canyons, whereas alluvial fans, bajadas, and dune fields are common in Death Valley.

Wind is effective in deserts because desert soils are not protected by vegetation. But wind is equally effective in other environments where vegetation is sparse, such as many coastal regions, where dunes and other wind-created landforms are also common.

A Focus On box describes desertification, expansion of a desert caused by human mismanagement. Here we discuss problems that can result from agriculture in semiarid regions. In other semiarid regions, human pressure takes forms other than agriculture. Over long weekends in the fall and winter, as many as 70,000 people may visit a narrow strip of sand dunes on the eastern edge of the Imperial Valley in California. Many ride motorcycles or dune buggies. The tire tracks disrupt vegetation and leave deep trenches in nearby playas.

Perhaps in the future, deserts will provide energy as well as minerals. In the Coachella Valley in southern California, 4,000 wind turbines generate electricity. In the Mojave desert, near Barstow California, electricity is generated from steam produced when sunlight is concentrated on a boiler from an array of heliostats. Electricity for one million homes could be generated from the sunlight incident on 20 square miles of southern California desert. If solar cells become economical, there will be pressure to develop much of this potential. If deserts are industrialized in this manner, the environmental impact on these fragile ecosystems will become significant.

Answers to Discussion Questions

1. The northwest coast of North America from Oregon to southeast Alaska supports coastal

rainforests. Here, warm moist Pacific Ocean air blows over a cool landscape and moisture condenses. In contrast, the Atacama desert, one of the driest in the world, lies on the west coast of South America in Peru and Chile. Here, cool ocean currents bring cool air to a warm land. When cool air is heated, the relative humidity decreases and no rain falls.

2. Soil moisture depends on both rainfall and rates of evaporation. In a region with intense sunlight, evaporation will be higher and soil moisture lower than in another region with the same rainfall but less sun. Because plants need water in the root zone to grow, soil moisture determines plant growth. In turn, an ecosystem is defined by the plants that grow in it. For example, the San Fernando Valley receives 65 centimeters of rain. However, most of this falls during the winter. During the summer, the hot sun and sparse rainfall combine to dry out the soil so that a portion of the region is nearly desert.

3. Formation of a mountain range can create a rain-shadow desert. Migration of a continent to the 30° high pressure zone can also create a desert environment.

4. Obviously it would be easy to prove that the landing site was <u>not</u> a desert if abundant vegetation were photographed and if the soil were rich in organic matter. However, we can imagine many sites where false interpretations could occur. If the spacecraft landed on a coastal dune in a humid environment, there would be little vegetation or organic matter. Similarly, exposed mountainous terrain, regions recently covered by young lava, or landscapes eroded by glaciers could be mistaken for deserts. You might learn little by measuring rainfall over a two week period. Dry periods occur in humid environments, and occasionally rainstorms occur in the desert. In order to perform a conclusive experiment, you would need a greater range of visibility, a longer lifetime for the spacecraft, or more test sites.

5. Because vegetation is sparse in deserts, soil and bare rock are exposed. In many deserts, the limited rain falls in short, intense storms. Under such conditions the water doesn't soak in, but rather flows across the bare surface, rapidly eroding soil and rock. Rapid flow over unprotected soil frequently causes mudflows, debris flows, and other forms of mass wasting in deserts.

6. Of the three agents of erosion, wind is the least viscous, ice is the most. As a result, wind cannot pick up anything larger than sand whereas streams may pick up cobbles and even boulders, and ice picks up giant boulders routinely. The same sequence occurs for transport; wind transports sand close to the ground and for short distances, but carries silt aloft. Streams transport sand more easily and at high flows may transport cobbles or boulders, while ice transports particles of all sizes. Wind travels across the surface of the land and deposits particles in any sheltered lee, whereas streams flow in channels for most of the year and deposit sediment

in bars and deltas. Glaciers can fill an entire valley and frequently deposit sediment in massive moraines.

7. Alluvial fans typically contain cobbles that are too large to be transported by the wind. Also alluvial fan deposits are typically poorly sorted, whereas wind deposits are well sorted.

8. (a) parabolic; (b) barchan.

9. A seacoast.

10. Ground water may seep downward through permeable gravel and other sediment of coalescing alluvial fans until it encounters impermeable bedrock. It then flows along the bedrock surface beneath the gravel until the bedrock is exposed at the land surface, where the water flows from a spring.

Selected Reading

Three good books on deserts and desert processes are:
Tony Allan and Andrew Warren, eds., *Deserts: The Encroaching Wilderness*. Oxford: Oxford University Press, 1993, 176 pages.

Ron Cooke, *Desert Geomorphology*. Cincinnati: UCL Press, 1993, 536 pages.

V P Tchakerian, *Desert Aeolian Processes*. New York: Chapman & Hall, 1995, 340 pages.

Several modern references on desertification are as follows:
H. E. Dregne, "Arid Land Degradation: A Result of Mismanagement." *Geotimes*, June 1991;

David S. G. Thomas and Nicholas J. Middleton, *World Atlas of Desertification*. New York: Chapman & Hall, 1992, 96 pages;

Lennart Olsson, "On the Causes of Famine-Drought, Desertification and Market Failure in the Sudan." *Ambio, 22*(6), 1991;

Compton J. Tucker, Harold E. Dregne, and Wilbur W. Newcomb, "Expansion and Contraction of the Sahara Desert from 1980 to 1990." *Science, 253*, July 19, 1991.

Dunes are discussed in:
Nicholas Landcaster, *The Geomorphology of Desert Dunes*. New York: Routledge, 1996, 290 pages.

Tom Waters, "Dunes." *Earth*, January 1993.

Chapter 12 Test

Multiple Choice:

1. Outside of the polar regions, the Earth's land surface is _____ desert
(a) about 25 percent (b) less than 3 percent (c) 50 percent (d) about 10 percent

2. Vast tropical rainforests grow near the equator because
(a) warm moist air sinks, creating low pressure; (b) warm, moist air rises to form a high pressure region; (c) rising air cools and condenses as rain; (d) rising air is heated and the moisture condenses.

3. Water vapor that has condensed over a mountain range is more likely to fall as rain and snow
(a) on the lee side of the range; (b) on the windward side of the range; (c) in a rain-shadow desert; (d) none of these.

4. Large desert rivers like the Colorado River receive most of their water from
(a) ground water reserves; (b) wetter, mountainous areas bordering the arid lands; (c) seasonal rains; (d) occasional, intense summer thunderstorms.

5. A _____ is a broad depositional surface formed by merging alluvial fans.
(a) bajada (b) pediment (c) butte (d) ventifact

6. Buttes and mesas are common in the Colorado Plateau because
(a) chemical weathering rounds the edges of rock outcrops; (b) through-flowing rivers transport sediment away from the area; (c) these landforms are composed of evaporite deposits; (d) these landforms commonly form at the base of bajadas.

7. Death Valley
(a) is a coastal desert; (b) is a rain-shadow desert; (c) has no water or plant life; (d) is drained by streams that flow through it to the ocean.

8. In the Great Basin of the western United States
(a) streams flow from the basin carrying sediment to the sea; (b) no streams flow into or away from the region; (c) sediment is filling the valleys because streams flow into the valleys from surrounding mountains, but no streams flow away from the region; (d) little sediment accumulates because much of the region is desert or semi-arid.

9. Erosion of soil by wind is
(a) saltation; (b) deflation; (c) inflation; (d) minimal in deserts; (e) augmented by plant cover.

10. Wind-scoured depressions are called
(a) alluvial fans; (b) blowouts; (c) kettles; (d) playas; (e) sinkholes.

11. Desert pavement forms because
(a) caliche deposits cement desert soil; (b) wind selectively removes sand and leaves large particles behind; (c) playa lake beds bake rock-hard in the hot summer sun; (d) all of the above.

12. The effects of abrasion by wind-blown sand and silt
(a) are concentrated close to the ground; (b) are responsible for the delicate caps on high desert pinnacles; (c) create caliche; (d) form playa lakes.

13. Wind erodes sand
(a) from the windward side of a dune, and deposits it on the sheltered lee side; (b) from the lee side of a dune, and deposits it on the windward side; (c) from both sides of a dune; (d) only from the top of a dune.

14. A crescent-shaped dune with tips pointing downwind that forms in area of little sand is a _____ dune.
(a) parabolic (b) transverse (c) barchan (d) longitudinal

15. Wind blows sand from a blowout and deposits it in a crescent-shaped dune with tips anchored by vegetation and pointing upwind to form a
(a) parabolic dune; (b) transverse dune; (c) barchan dune; (d) longitudinal dune; (e) stable dune.

16. In fossil dunes
(a) the numerous fossils form limestone; (b) the numerous fossils have been obliterated by wind action; (c) the dipping beds are the layering of the dune's slip face; (d) the dipping beds are the layering of the windward dune face.

17. The largest loess deposits in the world are found in
(a) New York; (b) Central China; (c) the North American Great Plains; (d) the Atacama Desert in Peru.

18. Overgrazing a semiarid region
(a) kills all the desert plants; (b) converts a semiarid land to a desert; (c) kills vegetation but increases the permeability and porosity of the soil; (d) changes the species distribution of plants.

True or False:

1. Two large desert zones encircle the globe 5 degrees north and south of the equator.

2. The Atacama Desert along the west coast of South America is so dry that, on the average, portions of Peru and Chile receive no rainfall for a decade or more.

3. The world's deserts are similar to one another only in that they all receive scant rainfall.

4. Deserts never occur along coastlines.

5. In the desert, the water table is often so low that water seeps from a stream bed into the ground below.

6. The day after a flash flood, a desert wash may contain only a tiny trickle, and within 24 hours it may be completely dry again.

7. Playa lakes remain wet the year round.

8. Because air is much less dense than water, wind can move only small particles, mainly silt and sand.

9. Windblown sand and silt are not effective agents of erosion.

10. Sand grains are usually lifted more than 1 meter in the air and are transported a long distance.

11. Migrating dunes can overrun buildings and highways.

12. When a barchan dune migrates, the edges move more slowly because there is more sand to transport.

13. Much of the rich soil of the central plains of the United States formed on loess.

14. Most dunes are asymmetrical.

15. Loess particles can interlock strongly enough that people can dig loess caves for homes.

16. Deserts can grow, shrink, and disappear over time.

Completion:

1. _____ _____ _____ form on the leeward sides of mountain range.

2. A/an _____ is a nearly flat, gently sloping surface eroded into bedrock along desert mountains.

3. An intermittent desert lake is called a _____ lake.

4. When wind blows, it removes only the small particles, leaving the pebbles and rocks to form a continuous cover of stones called _____ _____.

5. The Qattara Depression is an example of a large _____.

6. Cobbles and boulders with flat faces abraded by wind blown sand are called _____.

7. The leeward face of a dune is called the _____ _____.

8. A/an _____ dune forms if the wind direction is erratic but prevails from the same general direction and the supply of sand is limited.

9. Fossil dunes form when dunes are buried by other sediment and _____.

Answers for Chapter 12:

Multiple Choice: 1. a; 2. c; 3. b; 4. b; 5. a; 6. b; 7. b; 8. c; 9. b; 10. b; 11. b; 12. a; 13. a; 14. c; 15. a; 16. c; 17. b; 18. d

True or False: 1. F; 2. T; 3. T; 4. F; 5. T; 6. T; 7. F; 8. T; 9. F; 10. F; 11. T; 12. F; 13. T; 14. T; 15. T; 16. T

Completion: 1. Rain-shadow deserts; 2. pediment; 3. playa; 4. desert pavement; 5. blowout; 6. ventifacts; 7. slip face; 8. longitudinal; 9. lithified

CHAPTER 13

Ocean Basins

Discussion

In this chapter we use the plate tectonics concepts described in Chapter 5 to explain the geologic, topographic, and bathymetric features of the Earth's ocean basins. In turn, this discussion of the geology of the sea floor allows us to expand on the plate tectonics model.

We summarize the general characteristics of the world's oceans and ocean basins, and then describe methods of studying the sea floor, pointing out with Figure 13-5, that ocean basins have as much topographic (bathymetric) diversity as continents. Section 13.3 describes relationships between the Earth's magnetic field and sea floor magnetic patterns, and explains how sea floor magnetism led to the hypothesis of sea-floor spreading and, ultimately, to the plate tectonics theory.

The mid-oceanic ridge system is described as a world-encircling spreading center where new lithosphere and oceanic crust form. We then apply and amplify the plate tectonics model to describe the three layers of oceanic crust, and the nature and origins of continental margins, marine trenches, submarine canyons and abyssal fans, island arcs, seamounts, atolls, and oceanic islands.

One Focus On box describes life on the deep sea floor and black smokers. A second Focus On box explores the relationships among sea floor spreading rates, eustatic sea level changes, and deposition of marine sediments on continents.

Answers to Discussion Questions

1. The east coast of South America is a passive margin. Hence it has accumulated sediment to construct its shelf-slope-rise complex since the time it rifted from western Africa. In contrast, the western coast of South America is an active margin. Much of the sediment shed into the Pacific coast slides into the trench, and therefore does not accumulate on a stable margin to construct a broad shelf.

2. The junction between continental and oceanic crust is probably characterized by numerous normal faults, or half-grabens, in both the granitic and basaltic sides of the junction. They must have formed during rifting of continental crust, and continued to form as oceanic crust was added to the widening rift. The continental basement rock at the junction may be of any age, but the oceanic crust must have formed at the time rifting was initiated. Arkosic sandstones are probably

common near the junction as a result of active normal faulting during rifting. Evaporites are probably also common, because restricted seas were associated with a newly opening marine basin with poorly developed access to the open ocean.

The basaltic side of the junction probably is no thicker that normal oceanic crust. The granitic continental crust may thin to only about 10 kilometers as a result of erosion and normal faulting. In places, basalt flows must cover granitic crust as a result of volcanism associated with the beginning of rifting of the continent.

3. Most weathering, erosion, and sediment transport is caused by water. If there were no water, surface features would be altered by wind and mass wasting but rates of weathering and erosion would be much slower than at present. As a result, mountain ranges would be higher and more plateau-like, valleys and canyons less pronounced, and less sediment would accumulate in intracratonic basins and continental margins. However, the fundamental structure of ocean basins and continents would be the same as in the modern Earth.

If the entire surface were covered with water, there would still be differentiation into thick granitic and thinner basaltic crust. Surface erosion from streams and glaciers would not occur, so again the shape of mountain ranges and plains would be different.

4. Orogenic events most commonly build a mountain chain at a continental margin (although a continental collision traps the mountains between two colliding continents). Because a mountain chain is near an active continental margin, only relatively short streams flow from the mountain crest to the active margin. Long drainage systems commonly flow from the other side of the mountain chain to a passive margin, however, because the young mountains tend to be high, and form a continental drainage divide that is far from passive margins. Consider North America: short drainages flow eastward to the Atlantic from the Appalachians, and from the Cordillera westward to the Pacific. But very long drainages flow southwestward from the Appalachians and southeastward from the Cordillera to the Mississippi and the Gulf of Mexico.

Selected Reading

Several recent books provide excellent supplementary descriptions of the geology of the ocean basins:

William J. Broad, *The Universe Below: Discovering the Secrets of the Deep Sea.* New York: Simon and Schuster, 1997.

Richard Ellis, *Deep Atlantic: Life, Death, and Exploration in the Abyss.* New York: Knopf, 1996, 395 pages.

Kenneth J. Hsu, *Challenger at Sea: A Ship that Revolutionized Earth Science.* New Jersey: Princeton University Press, 1992, 417 pages.

Susan E. Humphris, Robert A. Zierenberg, Lauren S. Mullineaux, and Richard E. Thompson eds., *Seafloor Hydrothermal Systems, Physical, Chemical, Biological and Geological Interactions.* Washington: American Geophysical Union, 1995, 466 pages.

Adolphe Nicolas, *The Mid-Oceanic Ridges, Mountains Below Sea Level.* Berlin, Springer, 1995, 200 pp.

E. Seibold and W. H. Berger, *The Sea Floor, An Introduction to Marine Geology*, 3rd edition. Berlin: Springer 1993, 360 pages.

We also recommend two journal articles used to prepare this chapter:
Kenneth C. Macdonald and Paul J. Fox, "The Mid-Ocean Ridge." *Scientific American*, 6: 72-79, 1990.

Kenneth C. Macdonald, Daniel Scheirer, and Suzanne M. Carbotte, "Mid-Ocean Ridges: Discontinuities, Segments, and Giant Cracks." *Science, 253*: 986- 994, 1991.

Chapter 13 Test

Multiple Choice:

1. The oceans are about _____ deep above the abyssal plains between the mid-oceanic ridges and the edges of the continent.
(a) 10 kilometers (b) 5 kilometers (c) 350 meters (d) 2 kilometers (e) 3-4 miles

2. Samples can be taken from the deep sea floor by
(a) seismic profilers; (b) echo sounders; (c) coring devices; (d) remote sensing; (e) all of these.

3. When iron-bearing minerals cool in the Earth's magnetic field, they
(a) settle rapidly toward the Earth's core; (b) expand and become buoyant; (c) preserve a record of the orientation of the Earth's magnetic field at the time the mineral cooled; (d) refract at the mantle-core boundary.

4. When a magnetic reversal occurs
(a) the north magnetic pole becomes the south magnetic pole, and vice versa; (b) iron-bearing minerals in the sea floor lose their magnetism; (c) earthquakes occur as iron bearing minerals change direction; (d) a and b

5. The mid-oceanic ridge is composed mainly of
(a) granite; (b) ocean floor sediments; (c) folded and faulted sedimentary rocks; (d) basalt.

6. The mid-oceanic ridge rises high above the surrounding sea floor because
(a) new lithosphere forming at the ridge axis is hot and of relatively low density; (b) new lithosphere forming at the ridge axis is hot and of relatively high density; (c) new lithosphere forming at the ridge axis is cool and of relatively high density (d) new lithosphere forming at the ridge axis is cool and of relatively low density.

7. Oceanic crust is relatively young because
(a) it forms continuously at spreading centers and recycles into the mantle at subduction zones; (b) it cannot return to the mantle; (c) it sinks into the mantle at the rift valley; (d) it is made of basalt, which is the youngest rock on Earth; (e) none of these.

8. The part of oceanic crust made up of pelagic and terrigenous sediment is
(a) layer 1; (b) layer 2; (c) layer 3; (d) located beneath basalt layers; (e) the mafic zone.

9. Most of layer 2 of the oceanic crust is
(a) pelagic sediment; (b) pillow basalt; (c) gabbro; (d) terrigenous sediment; (e) basaltic dikes.

10. The remains of tiny plants and animals that settle to the sea floor collect to form
(a) zooplankton; (b) terrigenous sediment; (c) pelagic sediment; (d) pillow basalt; (e) gabbro.

11. The flattest surfaces on Earth are
(a) cratons; (b) mid-ocean ridges; (c) abyssal plains; (d) high plains; (e) continental shelves.

12. Continental crust and oceanic crust firmly join together at a/an
(a) mid-oceanic ridge; (b) passive continental margin; (c) active continental margin; (d) convergent plate boundary.

13. The continental rise on a passive continental margin is
(a) a rugged surface formed by erosion of sediment near the continental margin; (b) an apron of terrigenous sediment that was transported across the continental shelf and deposited on the deep ocean floor at the foot of the continental slope; (c) a topographic surface formed as a portion of a lithospheric plate dives into the mantle; (d) a steep surface formed by accumulation of basalt near the continental margin.

14. Submarine canyons on continental shelves and slopes are cut by
(a) black smokers; (b) longshore currents; (c) deep sea currents; (d) continental rivers and streams; (e) turbidity currents.

15. An active continental margin forms
(a) at mid-oceanic ridges; (b) at continent-continent margins; (c) where an oceanic plate sinks beneath a continental plate at a subduction zone; (d) in a rift valley; (e) at a black smoker.

16. An active continental margin commonly has a much narrower continental shelf and a considerably steeper continental slope than does a passive margin because
(a) undersea volcanoes form steep-sided slopes; (b) the subducting plate forms a steep-sided trench; (c) turbidity currents erode terrigenous sediment; (d) all of the above.

17. Island arcs grow from
(a) submarine volcanoes near a subduction zone; (b) passive continental margins; (c) atolls; (d) abyssal fans.

18. An oceanic island
(a) rises isostatically as it becomes older; (b) is a submarine volcano that forms above a hot spot or mantle plume (c) is a submarine volcano that forms adjacent to an oceanic trench and subduction zone; (d) is an atoll that forms above the mid-oceanic ridge.

19. Seawater heated near _____ and _____ can dissolve metals from oceanic crust, and deposit them as ore.
(a) the mid-oceanic ridge, submarine volcanoes (b) atolls, reefs (c) sea stacks, arches (d) abyssal plains, a passive continental margin (e) none of these

20. Chemical reactions between seawater and pelagic sediment form
(a) island arcs; (b) seamounts; (c) manganese nodules; (d) guyots.

True or False:

1. At present, the Atlantic Ocean is shrinking while the Pacific is growing.

2. Remote sensing methods require direct physical contact with the ocean floor.

3. The Earth's magnetic field has remained constant both in orientation and strength throughout geologic history.

4. Sea-floor basalt cannot be used to record the orientation of the Earth's magnetic field because it is rich in iron.

5. As new oceanic crust cools, it preserves a record of the orientation of the Earth's magnetic field at the time of cooling.

6. Shallow earthquakes commonly occur at the mid-oceanic ridge.

7. Basalt dikes and gabbro sills comprise Layer 1 of oceanic crust.

8. A continental shelf on a passive margin is always a narrow bathymetric feature.

9. Some of the world's richest offshore petroleum reserves are found on continental shelves.

10. A turbidity current can travel at speeds greater than 100 kilometers per hour and for

distances up to 700 kilometers.

11. Earthquakes are common at the mid-oceanic ridge and island arcs.

12. Seamounts and oceanic islands are volcanic peaks on the ocean floor.

13. If the Pacific Ocean plate continues to move at its present rate, the island of Hawaii may sink beneath the sea within 10 to 15 million years.

14. Hot seawater dissolves metals as it circulates through oceanic crust.

15. Manganese nodules are abundant both on the surface of and within ocean floor sediments.

Completion:

1. A/an _____ _____ is an open-mouthed steel net dragged along the sea floor behind a research ship.

2. The _____ _____ emits a sound signal from a research ship and then records the signal after it bounces off the sea floor.

3. The orientation of the Earth's field at present is referred to as normal, and that during a time of opposite polarity is
called _____.

4. The _____ _____ is a continuous submarine mountain chain that encircles the globe.

5. A _____ _____ is a deep trough in the crest of many mid-oceanic ridges.

6. _____ _____ is composed of sand, silt, and clay eroded from the continents and deposited on the ocean floor near continents by submarine currents.

7. Subduction of an oceanic plate beneath a continental plate occurs at a/an _____ _____ _____.

8. A/an _____ _____ is a shallow, gently sloping submarine surface on the submerged edge of a continent.

9. A steep region on the margin of a continental shelf that averages about 50 kilometers wide is the _____ _____.

10. Deep, V-shaped, steep-walled valleys called _____ _____ are eroded into continental shelves and slopes.

11. A long, narrow, steep-sided depression called a/an _____ forms on the sea floor where an oceanic plate bends downward as it sinks into the mantle.

12. A chain of volcanic islands that form along a subduction zone is called a(an) _____ _____.

13. A/an _____ is a submarine mountain that rises 1 kilometer or more above the surrounding sea floor.

14. The Hawaiian Islands are examples of _____ _____.

15. _____ _____ are jets of black metal-bearing solutions that spout from fractures in the mid-oceanic ridge.

Answers for Chapter 13

Multiple Choice: 1. b; 2. c; 3. c; 4. a; 5. d; 6. a; 7. a; 8. a; 9. b; 10. c; 11. c; 12. b; 13. b; 14. e; 15. c; 16. b; 17. a; 18. b; 19. a; 20. c

True or False: 1. F; 2. F; 3. F; 4. F; 5. T; 6. T; 7. F; 8. F; 9. T; 10. T; 11. T; 12. T; 13. T; 14. T; 15. F

Completion: 1. rock dredge; 2. echo sounder; 3. reversed; 4. mid-oceanic ridge; 5. rift valley; 6. Terrigenous sediment; 7. active continental margin; 8. continental shelf; 9. continental slope; 10. submarine canyons; 11. trench; 12. island arc; 13. seamount; 14. oceanic islands; 15. Black smokers

CHAPTER 14

Oceans and Coastlines

Discussion

The first part of this chapter introduces the chemistry of seawater, tides, waves, and currents. An interesting contrast exists between ocean waves and stream waves. If a stream flows swiftly over a rock, a wave forms over the rock. In this case, the wave doesn't move, but the water flows through it and continues downstream. In contrast, an ocean wave moves across the surface of the sea, but the water doesn't move along with the wave.

The material on vertical and horizontal ocean currents is an important prelude to climate discussions in Chapter 18. Scientists have long understood that surface currents, such as the Gulf Stream, transport heat from one region of the globe to another. However, the importance and delicate nature of vertical thermohaline circulation has not always been fully appreciated and is currently an active area of research.

The central theme of the second half of this chapter is that coastlines are among the most geologically active regions on the Earth. Weathering, erosion, transport, deposition, emergence, and submergence all alter coastal profiles. At the same time, coastlines are among the most desirable places to live. Therefore conflicts arise between human habitation and geologic change. After discussing the mechanisms of coastal geology, we introduce human development and pollution of coastal areas through two representative Case Studies: "Chesapeake Bay," and "Long Island."

The chapter ends with an introduction to sea level rise, a problem that could possibly become severe within the students' lifetimes. Focus On "Life in the Seas" provides a quick glance into the fascinating science of marine biology.

Answers to Discussion Questions

1. Wave properties were discussed in Chapter 6 under Earthquakes and again here in Chapter 14 under Coastlines. The repetition is intentional. All waves reflect, refract, and interfere (interference is not discussed in the text). Thus, earthquake waves in rock, ocean waves in water, and even electromagnetic waves in a vacuum behave in much the same manner. However all waves are not the same. A P wave is a compressional body wave in solid material or liquid. An S wave is a shear wave in a solid. Students find it confusing to say that different types of waves are different from one another and they affect the media in which they travel differently, yet they all reflect, refract, and interfere. Often they seek a simple answer, "Are different types of waves

the same or are they different?" The only accurate answer is: "Yes, they are the same, but they are also different."

2. The ship rides on the surface of the wave whereas waves break on the beach. If winds are strong enough, waves will break on the open ocean and these breaking waves cause the most damage to ships at sea.

3. The bottom of a wave encounters the sea floor when the depth diminishes to about one half the wavelength. Therefore the wavelength can be measured from aerial photos and the water depth can be determined from observations of surf.

4. Mid-ocean currents have little or no affect along shorelines, where most tanker accidents occur. Longshore currents, tides, and storm waves all disperse spilled oil. As a result it is important to act as quickly as possible when an accident occurs o contain and remove the oil. When the Exxon Valdez struck a rock near Valdez, Alaska, a delay of several days occurred before oil booms were deployed. Critics argue that this delay greatly magnified the effects of the spill because a lot of oil escaped. One solution would be to require all tankers to carry booms and other containment devices on board. These could then be deployed immediately with the ship's lifeboats.

5. In both coastlines and streams, moving water erodes rock and sediment by hydraulic action, abrasion, and solution. Sediment is then transported as dissolved load, suspended load, and bed load and then deposited where the water turbulence slows down.

     However, storm waves and surf are more turbulent than most stream flow. Stream beds are relatively narrow sinuous features with banks on either side whereas coastlines mark the edge of continents. Students may make other contrasts: For example floods and storm surges behave differently and salty ocean water weathers rock by salt cracking whereas river water contains a much smaller salt concentration.

6. Tectonic activity and sea level changes constantly alter coastlines. The same question could also apply to mountain ranges. We could ask, "If mountains are being eroded, why do they still exist?"

7. Most of the sediment along the east coast originated as moraine deposits in Long Island and was transported southward by longshore currents.

8. The government should support the construction of groins: The government has an interest in protecting commerce and the lives of its citizens. Coastal stabilization, flood control projects,

soil conservation, and avalanche control along highways all fall under this category.

The government should outlaw groins: In the long run, groins cause more erosion than they prevent. Furthermore, if one person builds a groin, he or she is effectively stealing the neighbor's beach and the government has a right to prevent one citizen from harming another.

The government should permit people to construct groins on their own property: The government should not interfere with peoples' lives or tell them want they can or cannot build on their own property.

9. As mentioned above, the government has an obvious interest in protecting commerce and the lives of its citizens. Various types of disaster relief are a form of national insurance. It is virtuous to help people who suffer losses from hurricanes, floods, drought, earthquakes, volcanic eruptions, or other natural disasters. Furthermore, disaster relief speeds the return to normal commerce and therefore helps the economy. An opposing argument is that it is common knowledge that barrier islands are geologically unstable, are prone to erosion, and are vulnerable to storms. In most areas, only wealthy people can afford waterfront property. Why should the government protect rich people who court disaster by building in especially vulnerable regions?

10. One social solution would be to eliminate construction of sea walls and groins and accept natural erosion and deposition. Some structures would be lost. Perhaps a national coastline park and wildlife refuge could be established. One technical solution would be to build bigger and better groin systems or sea walls. Even though we recognize that over the long term, many coastal management projects do more harm than good, in some instances they protect the coast in the short term. The technical argument is based on the assumption that if we are willing to pay the price, engineering projects can provide an effective, although temporary, barrier against the sea.

11. We wrote this question to emphasize how relief affects the character of a beach. (a) It wouldn't advance at all, just rise 25 cm up the cliff; (b) 35 cm along the slope of the beach; (c) 2.9 meters; (d) 14.4 meters.

12. Sea water density changes nearly linearly with water temperature. However, water temperature doesn't necessarily change in a linear relationship with air temperature. The deep ocean water, especially, is well insulated from the air. In addition, many other factors besides water temperature, discussed in the text, cause changes in sea level.

13. An example of this type of interaction is given in Section 18.5 in the Chapter on Climate Change.

Selected Reading

Two oceanography texts are:
Paul Pinet, *Oceanography, An Introduction to the Planet Oceanus*, St.Paul, MN: West Publishing, 1992, 551 pages.

M. Grant Gross, *Oceanography. 6th ed.*, New Jersey: Prentice-Hall, 1993, 446 pages.

Coastlines and their management are important topics discussed in:
Timothy Beatley, et al., *An Introduction to Coastal Zone Management*. Washington, D.C.: Island Press, 1994, 456 pages;

Charles I. Coultas and Yuch Ping Hsieh, eds., *Ecology and Management of Tidal Marshes, A Model from the Gulf of Mexico*. Boca Raton, FL: Lewis Publishers, 1997, 376 pages.

O.H. Pilkey, J.T. Kelly, and R.A. Morton, eds., *Coastal Land Loss and the US, The Causes and Case Histories*, New York: Chapman & Hall, 1995, 450 pages.

Carl J. Sindermann, *Ocean Pollution: Effects on Living Resources and Humans*. Boca Raton, FL: CRC Press, 1996, 304 pages.

An important source for material on Chesapeake Bay is:
Tom Horton and William M. Eichbaum, *Turning the Tide, Saving the Chesapeake Bay*. Washington, D.C.: Island Press, 1991, 324 pages.

Sea level is discussed in:
Lynne T. Edgerton, *The Rising Tide: Global Warming and World Sea Levels*. Washington, D.C.: Covelo Press, 1991, 136 pages.

K. O. Emery and David G. Aubrey, *Sea Levels, Land Levels and Tide Gauges*. New York: Springer-Verlag, 1991, 237 pages; and

Reefs are discussed in:
Jeremy Stafford-Deitsch, *A Safari through the Coral World*. San Francisco: Sierra Club Books, 1991, 200 pages.

A classic example of ocean pollution is:

Art Davidson, *In the Wake of the Exxon Valdez*, San Francisco: Sierra Club Books, 1990. 333 pages.

Chapter 14 Test

Multiple Choice:

1. The Sea of Cortez lies in a subtropical region between the Baja Peninsula and the west coast of Mexico. Most of the surrounding land is desert and the one large river, the Colorado, empties only a small amount of water into the sea. In contrast, the Straits of Georgia lies off the temperate coast of British Columbia and is fed by melting glaciers and many streams. Which of the following comparisons of the salinities of these regions is correct?
(a) The Straits of Georgia is saltier because the numerous rivers transport salt water into the sea; (b) The Straits of Georgia is saltier because cool temperatures promote salt crystallization; (c) The Sea of Cortez is saltier because fresh water input is low and evaporation is high; (d) Both regions have the same salinity because all the oceans are interconnected and the salt is evenly dispersed.

2. The thermocline
(a) is the upper warm surface of the ocean; (b) is the middle layer of the ocean where temperature drops rapidly with depth; (c) is the deep cold portion of the ocean; (d) does not exist near the equator where the ocean is hottest.

3. A neap tide is a
(a) small tide formed when the Sun and Moon are $90°$ out of alignment; (b) large tide formed when the Sun and Moon are $90°$ out of alignment; (c) small tide formed when the Sun and Moon are aligned; (d) large tide formed when the Sun and Moon are aligned.

4. Currents
(a) are continuous flows of water in a particular direction; (b) travel in circles, ending up where they started; (c) are found only near coastlines; (d) are found only near closely spaced islands; (e) are found only in the central oceans.

5. If an ocean current is flowing southward from the equator, it is moving eastward _____ than the water at higher latitudes and therefore veers to the _____.
(a) faster, east; (b) faster, west; (c) slower, east; (d) slower, west.

6. If surface water becomes most dense when it becomes
(a) warm and salty; (b) warm and less salty; (c) cool and salty; (d) cool and less salty.

7. Ocean waves steepen near shore because
(a) they speed up; (b) the wave length increases; (c) the lower portion of the wave slows down as it drags against the sea floor; (d) the lower part of the wave speeds up as it reflects off the sea floor.

8. If waves strike shore at an angle, they _____ and create a/an _____ that flows parallel to the beach.
(a) refract, longshore current (b) refract, tidal current (c) speed up, longshore; (d) speed up, tidal current.

9. The foreshore is the
(a) region below the low tide mark; (b) low tide mark; (c) region between the high and low tide lines; (d) region between the normal high tide line and the storm tide.

10. Coral reefs develop in
(a) shallow, tropical seas; (b) silty places; (c) cold oceans; (d) areas with little sunlight

11. A submergent coastline forms where
(a) sea level falls or coastal land sinks; (b) sea level falls or coastal land rises; (c) sea level rises or coastal land sinks; (d) sea level rises or coastal land rises

12. Most emergent coastlines are:
(a) sediment poor and likely to contain cliffs and sea stacks; (b) sediment poor and likely to contain barrier islands and spits; (c) sediment rich and likely to contain cliffs and sea stacks; (d) sediment rich and likely to contain barrier islands and spits.

13. The two essential ingredients for barrier island formation are
(a) a lack of sediment and waves or currents to erode coastal cliffs; (b) a large supply of sediment and waves or currents to transport the sediment along the coast; (c) an irregular coastline and offshore currents; (d) groins and stabilized beaches.

14. A groin
(a) is a type of sea wall that prevents waves from crashing against the beach; (b) prevents erosion by interrupting the flow of sand along the beach; (c) increases erosion by interrupting the flow of sand along a beach; (d) prevents erosion by stopping the movement of longshore currents; (e) increases erosion by deflecting deep water currents to the beach.

15. During the past 40,000 years, sea level has fluctuated by
(a) 10 meters; (b) 1000 meters; (c) 150 meters; (d) 150 centimeters.

True or False:

1. The salinity of the oceans has increased steadily throughout geologic time because rivers transport salt to the oceans.

2. There is one high tide a day that forms when a point on the Earth lies directly under the Moon.

3. In the polar regions, near-surface ocean water becomes saltier when the surface water freezes.

4. A wave breaks when the wave steepens and the crest rides over the trough.

5. An ocean wave moves along the sea surface, but the water in the wave travels in circular paths.

6. Most sediment found on a coast is produced by erosion at that location.

7. In an emergent coastline, a portion of the continental shelf that was previously underwater becomes exposed as dry land.

8. Emergent coasts commonly have steep, rocky shorelines.

9. A barrier island is a common feature of sediment-poor coastlines.

10. Longshore currents along the eastern coast of the United States carry an average of 2000 tons of sand a day past a given point.

11. Chesapeake Bay is an estuary formed by submergence of the Susquehanna River valley.

12. Sea level has risen and fallen repeatedly in the geologic past, and coastlines have emerged and submerged throughout the history of the planet.

Completion:

1. The _____ is the distance between successive crests or troughs of a wave.

2. When deep ocean water rises to the surface, the upward flow is called a/an _____.

3. Once a wave breaks, its water flows toward the beach as a chaotic, turbulent mass called _____.

4. A/an _____ is a continuous flow of water in a particular direction.

5. A/an _____ is any strip of shoreline washed by waves and tides.

6. A/an _____ is a wave-resistant ridge or mound built by corals, algae, and other organisms.

7. If a coastline rises or sea level falls a/an _____ coastline is created.

8. A long ridge of sand or gravel extending out from a beach is called a/an _____.

9. A sheltered body of water between the shore and a barrier island is a/an _____.

10. If waves cut a cave into a narrow headland, the cave may eventually erode all the way through the headland, forming a/an _____ _____.

11. A/an _____ is a narrow, steep-sided bay surrounded by high rocky cliffs or mountainous slopes.

12. _____ are the richest protein-producing environments on Earth.

Answers for Chapter 14

Multiple Choice: 1. c; 2. b; 3. a; 4. a; 5. a; 6. c; 7. c; 8. a; 9. c; 10. a; 11. c; 12. d; 13. b; 14. c; 15. c

True or False: 1. F; 2. F; 3. T; 4. T; 5. T; 6. F; 7. T; 8. F; 9. F; 10. T; 11. T; 12. T

Completion: 1. wavelength; 2. upwelling; 3. surf; 4. current; 5. beach; 6. reef; 7. emergent; 8. spit; 9. lagoon; 10. sea arch; 11. fjord 12. Estuaries

CHAPTER 15

The Earth's Atmosphere

Discussion

Chapter 15 discusses the composition and structure of the atmosphere, laying the groundwork for discussions of weather, climate, climate change, and air pollution in the following four chapters. We open the chapter with a discussion of atmospheric composition, and the factors that affect atmospheric pressure. If students understand that the Earth's atmosphere is different from those of its neighbors, Venus and Mars, and if they study the past interactions between living organisms and atmospheric composition, they will better appreciate concerns such as the depletion of stratospheric ozone and the greenhouse effect.

We discuss radiation and energy transfer in the atmosphere as a prelude to describing the greenhouse effect. These sections are followed by discussions of temperature changes with elevation, latitude, and seasons, and with an introduction to atmospheric heat transport and storage.

Two Focus On boxes describing "The Upper Fringe of the Atmosphere" and "Latitude and Longitude" supplement text materials in the chapter.

Answers to Discussion Questions

1. Pressure would decrease and initially the atmosphere would become thicker, ie its volume would increase to accommodate the decrease in pressure. However, with reduced gravity, many of the gases would eventually escape into space, leading to a permanent loss of much of the atmosphere.

2. The Sun emits a wide range of electromagnetic frequencies, including high energy ultraviolet, X-rays, and gamma radiation that are harmful to human beings. Therefore, astronauts must wear protective clothing in outer space. Most of the high energy rays (and many low ones) are absorbed in the upper atmosphere and do not reach the surface of the Earth. Therefore, people on the Earth do not need to wear such protective clothing.

3. There is more high frequency, high energy light on a mountain top than at sea level because many of these rays have not yet been absorbed in their passage through the atmosphere to the surface of the Earth. Sunburn is caused only by more energetic photons, you can sit all day in a warm room in front of a hot stove and not get a trace of a burn.

4. Snow has a high albedo and reflects most of the heat back into the atmosphere. Trees, twigs, and rocks absorb sunlight and become warm, thereby melting adjacent snow.

5. Alaska is so far north that in winter the sunlight strikes the Earth at a low angle even at noon, analogous to sunrise and sunset at lower latitudes.

6. (a) 47 percent (b) Although climate changes with time, these changes occur slowly and usually represent only a few degrees variation. Since large amounts of solar radiation are absorbed, and temperature remains relatively constant, heat must be re-radiated from the ground. The Earth absorbs short wavelength visible and UV radiation and re-radiates the same amount of energy at longer wavelengths.

7. The sunlight at the poles arrives at a low angle and is therefore less concentrated than the sunlight at the Equator.

8. If a lake froze in winter, its albedo and heat storage capacities would become very much like snowy land surfaces, and the lake would have little effect on local climate. If, however, the lake remained unfrozen, its heat transport and storage would be similar to that of the ocean, as explained in the text. Thus, deep lakes that don't freeze affect the climate in their immediate vicinity.

9. If oxygen and nitrogen absorbed visible radiation, the atmosphere would be opaque to sunlight and the upper atmosphere would be extremely hot. Life could not exist on the surface of the Earth. If oxygen and nitrogen absorbed infrared radiation, it would absorb radiation emitted from the ground and the Earth would become unbearably hot. However, the present atmospheric composition would never have evolved, because living organisms would not have evolved, or if evolution had started, life would have died out as the Earth heated.

10. The answers to this question are summarized in Section 17.1 of Chapter 17, and elaborated upon in most of the rest of Chapter 17. However, most of the fundamental information necessary to discuss the issue of Earth systems interactions and climate is found in Chapter 15. We hope that this discussion will prepare and interest the student in the following chapters.

11. If the Earth had no oceans, marine currents would not transfer heat from equatorial latitudes to polar ones, and the tropics would suffer much warmer climates while polar regions would be even colder than they are. No coastal climatic moderation would occur in the absence of oceans. Because the seas have a relatively low albedo, more solar heat would be reflected back into space

if ocean surfaces were replaced by land, and the Earth would cool.

If the spin axis were perpendicular to the plane of Earth's orbit, seasonal temperature variations would not exist. If the spin axis were tilted at 50° to the orbital plane, seasonal variations would be accentuated. Because seasonal temperature variations can affect glacial growth, and because ice has a high albedo, threshold and feedback climatic mechanisms might be triggered by variations in the Earth's orbital tilt.

Selected Reading

The chemistry and composition of our atmosphere are discussed further in:
John W. Birks, Jack G. Calvert, and Robert W. Sievers, eds., *The Chemistry of the Atmosphere: Its Impact on Global Change*. Washington: American Chemical Society, 1993, 180 pages.

P. Brimblecome, *Air Composition and Chemistry, Second Edition*. New York: Cambridge University Press, 1995, 267 pages.

Hanwant B. Singh, *Composition, Chemistry, and Climate of the Atmosphere*. New York: Van Nostrand Reinhold, 1995.

Two interesting books about changes in the chemical composition of the atmosphere are:
T. E. Graedel and Paul J. Crutzen, *Atmospheric Change, An Earth Systems Science Perspective*. New York: W. H. Freeman, 1992.

John H. Seinfeld and Spyros N. Pandis, *Atmospheric Chemistry and Physics, From Air Pollution to Climate Change*. New York: John Wiley, 1997, 360 pages.

Chapter 15 Test

Multiple Choice:

1. The Earth's original atmosphere
(a) contained oxygen as a major constituent; (b) was an effective filter that absorbed high energy ultraviolet rays; (c) would be poisonous to most forms of life today; (d) was formed by biological processes.

2. The Earth's modern atmosphere
(a) is composed of 80 percent oxygen; (b) does not filter high energy ultraviolet rays; (c) is similar to that found on Venus; (d) is composed of 78 percent nitrogen.

3. As early organisms evolved and multiplied, they released more _____ into the atmosphere.
(a) oxygen; (b) hydrogen; (c) nitrogen; (d) argon; (e) glucose

4. The modern concentration of 21 percent molecular oxygen in our atmosphere resulted largely from
(a) meteorite impacts; (b) biological activity; (c) tectonic activity; (d) the big bang theory.

5. The most abundant constituent of air is
(a) nitrogen; (b) oxygen; (c) helium; (d) water vapor; (e) methane.

6. The atmosphere
(a) becomes more dense with increasing altitude; (b) becomes less dense with increasing altitude; (c) remains at constant density with increasing altitude; (d) becomes less dense throughout the troposphere and then more dense in the stratosphere.

7. In a barometer the weight of the atmosphere, is compared with that of
(a) an equal column of nitrogen; (b) an equal column of oxygen; (c) a densely packed cylinder; (d) a vacuum.

8. Which is not an electromagnetic wave?
(a) light; (b) sound; (c) radio waves; (d) X-rays; (e) infrared rays

9. Radiation with long wavelength and low frequency
(a) is high energy radiation; (b) is low energy radiation; (c) has the same energy as all other forms of radiation; (d) is X-rays.

10. When an object absorbs radiation,
(a) the photons disappear and convert to another form of energy; (b) the energy is lost; (c) the photons reflect out to space; (d) the photons slow down; (e) the photons speed up.

11. The sky appears blue because
(a) Earth's atmosphere scatters blue and violet wavelengths through the sky; (b) light is reflected by the Earth's oceans; (c) there is no atmosphere to scatter the light in the uppermost atmosphere; (d) only blue frequencies are transmitted by the Sun; (e) none of these.

12. If scientists were to spread a thin layer of ashes on the Antarctic ice cap, we would expect that the albedo of the region would
(a) increase leading to warming of the region; (b) increase leading to regional cooling; (c) decrease leading to regional warming; (d) decrease leading to regional cooling.

13. _____ percent of the incoming solar radiation reaches Earth's surface.
(a) 1 percent (b) 99 percent; (c) 8 percent; (d) 47 percent; (e) 80 percent

14. Why doesn't Earth get hot enough to boil oceans and melt rocks from the radiant energy it absorbs from the Sun?
(a) The energy disappears. (b) The atmosphere cools the Earth. (c) The Sun sets at night. (d) The Earth re-radiates all the energy it absorbs from the Sun. (e) The oceans keep the Earth cool.

15. The Earth remains warm at night because
(a) the albedo absorbs and retains much of the radiation emitted by the Earth's surface; (b) the atmosphere absorbs and retains much of the radiation emitted from the Earth's surface; (c) the atmosphere absorbs and retains much of the radiation emitted by the Moon; (d) dark sky retains more heat than blue sky; (e) none of these.

16. Which of the following orders of the layers of the atmosphere is correct? (Start with the lowest layer)
(a)thermosphere < stratosphere < troposphere < mesosphere; (b) troposphere < mesosphere < stratosphere < thermosphere; (c) stratosphere < troposphere < mesosphere < thermosphere; (d) troposphere < stratosphere < mesosphere < thermosphere.

17. The temperature of the stratosphere increases with elevation because the stratosphere
(a) is heated primarily by the Earth; (b) is heated primarily by solar radiation; (c) is located closer to the equator; (d) is closer to the Earth's surface; (e) none of these.

18. The region of the globe directly beneath the Sun is warmer because
(a) it receives the most concentrated radiation; (b) it receives the least concentrated radiation; (c) it receives light of a different frequency; (d) it receives light of a different wavelength.

19. Atmospheric convection and advection
(a) are less effective than conduction in transferring heat around the globe; (b) are more effective than conduction in transferring heat around the globe; (c) are about equally effective as conduction in transferring heat around the globe; (d) are unimportant processes in transferring heat around the globe.

20. _____ plays an important role in heat transfer and storage because it commonly occurs naturally on Earth in all three states, solid, liquid, and gas.
(a) Hydrogen; (b) Air; (c) Water; (d) Rock; (e) Soil

21. If you place a pan of water and a rock outside on a hot summer day,
(a) the rock becomes hotter than the water; (b) the water becomes hotter than the rock; (c) the rock and the water heat to equal temperatures; (d) the rock receives a larger quantity of solar radiation; (e) none of these

True or False:

1. If you landed on the Moon without a space suit, you would not live long.

2. As early organisms evolved and multiplied, they released more oxygen into the atmosphere.

3. If all life on Earth were to cease, the atmosphere would revert to its primitive, oxygen-poor composition and become poisonous to modern plants and animals.

4. The amount of radiation that the Earth receives from the Sun is so small that it hardly warms the Earth's surface.

5. Photons appear when they are emitted and disappear when they are absorbed.

6. Visible light is a large portion of the electromagnetic spectrum.

7. Radiation can travel through space with no change in wavelength or loss of energy.

8. The Earth emits higher energy radiation than the Sun does.

9. If Earth had no atmosphere, sunlight would travel directly to the surface and the Sun would look white in a black sky.

10. If the air is filled with dust or water droplets, all the wavelengths scatter and the sky becomes red.

11. If the Earth's albedo were to rise by growth of glaciers or increase in cloud cover, the surface of our planet would warm.

12. If Earth had no atmosphere, radiant heat loss would be so rapid that the Earth's surface would cool drastically at night.

13. The ozone in the upper atmosphere protects life on Earth by absorbing much of the high-energy radiation before it reaches Earth's surface.

14. All areas of the globe receive the same total number of hours of sunlight every year.

15. Air is a good conductor of heat.

16. Continental interiors are commonly cooler in summer and warmer in winter than coastal areas.

Completion:

1. _____ is the state of the atmosphere at a given place and time.

2. _____ is a composite of weather patterns from season to season, averaged over many years.

3. Fires burn rapidly where _____ is abundant, so if its concentration were to increase even by a few percent, fires would burn uncontrollably across the planet.

4. The pressure exerted by air is the _____ _____.

5. Particles of light are called _____.

6. The _____ _____ is the continuum of radiation of different wavelengths.

7. The Earth's surface emits _____ radiation, which has relatively long wavelength and low frequency.

8. Atmospheric gases, water droplets, and dust particles _____ sunlight in all directions.

9. _____ is the reflectivity of a surface.

10. The _____ traps heat radiating from Earth and acts as an insulating blanket.

11. The layer of air closest to the Earth, the layer we live in, is the _____.

12. Little radiation is absorbed in the _____, and the thin air is extremely cold.

13. On the _____ every portion of the globe receives 12 hours of sunlight and 12 hours of darkness.

14. _____ is the transport of heat by collisions between atoms and molecules.

15. _____ and _____ are the transport of heat by currents in liquids or gases.

16. _____ _____ is the energy released or absorbed when a substance changes from one state to another.

17. _____ _____ is the amount of energy needed to raise the temperature of 1 gram of material by 1° C.

Answers for Chapter 15

Multiple Choice: 1. c; 2. d; 3. a; 4. b; 5. a; 6. b; 7. d; 8. b; 9. b; 10. a; 11. a; 12. c; 13. d; 14. d; 15. b; 16. d; 17. b; 18. a; 19. b; 20. c; 21. a

True or False: 1. T; 2. T; 3. T; 4. F; 5. T; 6. F; 7. T; 8. F; 9. T; 10. F; 11. F; 12. T; 13. T; 14. F; 15. F; 16. F.

Completion: 1. Weather; 2. Climate; 3. oxygen; 4. barometric pressure; 5. photons; 6. electromagnetic spectrum; 7. infrared; 8. scatter; 9. Albedo; 10. atmosphere; 11. troposphere; 12. mesosphere; 13. equinox; 14. Conduction; 15. Convection and advection; 16. Latent heat; 17. Specific heat.

CHAPTER 16

Weather

Discussion

Most students watch weather reports on TV and have learned generalizations, such as low pressure systems bring rain and high pressure brings sunshine. They have heard terms such as cold fronts, warm fronts, and jet stream and have watched the sky as stratus clouds bring steady rain or cumulus clouds build on a summer afternoon to towering thunderheads. In this chapter we explain these relationships. The weather is defined primarily by moisture and wind. Therefore we start the chapter with a discussion of moisture in air: humidity, clouds, and precipitation, and follow with pressure and wind. With this background, the student can understand the winds and rainfall that occur when air masses collide, creating frontal weather systems, and the effects of mountains, oceans, and large lakes on weather. The chapter ends with a discussion of violent storms: thunderstorms, tornadoes, and tropical cyclones.

Chapter 16 contains Focus On Boxes explaining El Nino and describing Cloud Seeding.

Answers to Discussion Questions

1.

Temperature	Amount of water when air is saturated (g/m^3)	Amount of water at 50 % relative humidity (g/m^3)
0° C	4.8	2.4
10° C	9.4	4.7
20° C	17.3	8.6
40° C	51.2	25.6

2. Frost forms when vapor-laden air inside the refrigerator
comes in contact with the cooling coils. More frost would form in summer in a humid region where the outside air is warm and moist.

3. The greatest amount of condensation occurs when the maximum amount of moisture evaporates into the air during the day and the temperature difference between night and day is greatest. Condition (a) would not lead to condensation, (b) would produce dew, (c) would produce frost.

4. Students can construct this chart using the information contained in Section 16-3.

5. Wind is powered by the Sun's energy. Thus wind is a heat engine and obeys the same thermodynamic laws as any heat engine such as an automobile engine or a steam fired turbine.

6. A sunny day because the Sun warms the Earth creating temperature differences between ground and sea. Also, the ground radiates heat faster on a clear night than on a cloudy night and therefore cools more.

7. An air mass is a large body of air with approximately uniform temperature and humidity at any given altitude. Typically, an air mass is 1500 kilometers or more across and several kilometers thick. Because air acquires both heat and moisture from the Earth's surface, an air mass is classified by its place of origin. As explained in the text, such a collision produces low pressure and rain. The characteristics of the storm depend on the relative velocities, temperature, and moisture content of the two air masses.

8. The answer to this question depends upon the locality and the weather prediction in the newspaper.

9. Section 16.9 and the Focus On Box "El Nino" describe the effects of weather on humans, crops, and animals. The following two chapters describing climate and climate changes discuss the effects that humans, plants, and animals can have on climate, and therefore, on weather.

Selected Reading

Four books on weather are:
W.J. Burroughs, *Watching the World's Weather*. Cambridge: Cambridge University Press, 1991. 196 pages.

Jack Fishman and Robert Kalish, *The Weather Revolution: Innovations and Imminent Breakthroughs in Accurate Forecasting*. New York: Plenum, 1994, 276 pages.

J.F.R. McIlveen, *Fundamentals of Weather and Climate*. New York: Chapman & Hall, 1991, 544 pages.

Frederik Nebeker, *Calculating The Weather: Meteorology in the 20th Century*. New York: Academic, 1995, 255 pages.

Some new references on extreme weather events are:
Gary A. England, *Weathering the Storm: Tornadoes, Television, and Turmoil*. Norman, OK: University of Oklahoma Press, 1996, 225 pages.

David E. Fisher, *The Scariest Place on Earth: Eye to Eye with Hurricanes*. New York: Random, 1994, 250 pages.

David Laskin, *Braving the Elements: The Stormy History of American Weather*. New York: Anchor, 1996, 241 pages.

Several books to help students understand weather reports, maps, and charts are:
Peter R. Chaston, *Weather Maps: How to Read and Interpret all the Basic Weather Charts*. London: Chaston Scientific, 1995, 167 pages.

Ronald L. Wagner and Bill Adler, Jr., *The Weather Sourcebook: Your One-Stop Resource for Everything You Need to Feed Your Weather Habit*. Old Saybrook, CT: Globe Pequot, 1994, 210 pages.

David M. Ludlum, *The Audubon Society Field Guide to North American Weather*. New York: Knopf, 1991. 656 pages.

An interesting book about El Nino is:
Michael Glantz, *Currents of Change El Nino's Imapct on Climate and Society*. New York: Cambridge University Press, 1996, 207 pages.

Chapter 16 Test

Multiple Choice:

1. Which of the following statements about atmospheric humidity is correct?
(a) Cold air can hold more moisture than warm air. (b) Rain or fog is likely to occur when cool moist air is heated. (c) Dew forms when warm moist air comes in contact with cool surfaces. (d) Fog occurs when warm moist air from the ocean blows over warmer land surfaces.

2. _____ _____ is the amount of water vapor in air compared to the maximum it can hold at a given temperature.
(a) Relative humidity; (b) Absolute humidity; (c) Dew point; (d) Adiabatic lapse rate; (e) Partial humidity

3. Moisture condenses from air when the air
(a) loses heat by radiation and cools; (b) gains heat by radiation and warms; (c) warms adiabatically as it sinks to a lower elevation; (d) cools adiabatically as it sinks to a lower elevation.

4. Which of the following processes would lower the relative humidity of a parcel of air?
(a) The air moves over a lake where water is evaporating. (b) The air is heated and no water enters or leaves the system. (c) The air cools and no water enters or leaves. (d) Dust blows into the air but no other changes occur.

5. Which of the following conditions is likely to lead to rain?
(a) warm, moist air rises; (b) cool, moist air falls; (c) warm air makes contact with cool surfaces; (d) moist air sinks as it passes over the lee side of a mountain

6. Supercooled droplets do not freeze because
(a) there are too many particles to condense onto; (b) they are not cold enough; (c) there are no solid particles to condense onto; (d) they have a natural antifreeze in them; (e) none of these.

7. During an adiabatic temperature change
(a) air is heated by the sun; (b) air is cooled by the polar ice caps; (c) air cools by evaporation; (d) the temperature rises or falls as air pressure changes.

8. Once clouds start to form, rising air

(a) cools more quickly than it did lower in the atmosphere; (b) heats up; (c) no longer cools as rapidly as it did lower in the atmosphere; (d) turns into rain; (e) none of these.

9. If air stops rising before it cools to its dew point,
(a) clouds form; (b) no clouds form; (c) it rains; (d) it snows; (e) none of these.

10. When condensation occurs at the same elevation at which air stops rising,
(a) cumulus clouds form; (b) cirrus clouds form; (c) stratus clouds form; (d) no clouds form; (e) all of these.

11. Rain doesn't fall from all clouds because
(a) some contain water droplets so small that they evaporate before they reach Earth's surface; (b) some contain no water droplets; (c) some contain water droplets that are too large to fall; (d) none of these.

12. If one portion of the atmosphere becomes warmer than surrounding air,
(a) the warm air expands and rises; (b) a high pressure forms; (c) clouds disappear; (d) the warm air contracts and falls; (e) none of these.

13. Sinking air exerts a downward force to form a
(a) low-pressure region; (b) high-pressure region; (c) rainstorm; (d) hurricane; (e) orographic region.

14. Since warm air can hold more moisture than cold air, clouds generally do not form over
(a) low-pressure regions; (b) high-pressure regions; (c) mountains; (d) the seashore; (e) none of these.

15. If a large pressure difference occurs over a short distance
(a) there is little wind; (b) it rains; (c) it snows; (d) wind blows rapidly; (e) wind blows slowly.

16. A high altitude wind system traveling south from the Equator toward the South Pole
(a) would not be affected by the Earth's spin, because only surface winds are deflected; (b) would be deflected to the east by the Earth's spin; (c) would be deflected to the west by the Earth's spin; (d) would be accelerated southward by the Earth's spin.

17. Orographic lifting creates abundant precipitation on the
(a) leeward side of a mountain range; (b) on the crest and windward side of a mountain range; (c) in the rain shadow zone; (d) over the nearest large body of water.

18. When a warm air mass overtakes a cool one
(a) the cool air rises, leading to precipitation; (b) the cool air rises, leading to fair weather; (c) the warm air rises, leading to precipitation; (d) the warm air rises, leading to fair weather.

19. Monsoons
(a) blow from land to sea in early summer bringing drought; (b) blow from sea to land when the Earth cools, bringing rain; (c) blow from sea to land in summer bringing rain; (d) blow from land to sea in summer bringing rain.

20. Tropical cyclones
(a) form only over warm oceans; (b) form over any ocean; (c) form only over cold oceans ; (d) intensify as they pass from the sea onto land.

True or False:

1. Warm air can hold less water vapor than cold air.

2. Rain is almost always caused by cooling that occurs when air rises.

3. If dry air were to rise from sea level to 9000 meters (about the height of Mount Everest), it would cool by 90°C (162°F).

4. Rising air warms adiabatically.

5. Evaporation fogs are common in late fall and early winter, when the air has become cool but the water is still warm.

6. About one million cloud droplets must combine to form an average-size raindrop.

7. Hail falls only from stratus clouds.

8. When a mass of cool air comes in contact with warm air the cool air rises over the warm air.

9. Wind always flows from a region of high pressure toward a low-pressure region.

10. Pressure gradients change slowly, once or twice a year.

11. The jet stream caused U.S. bombers to miss their targets on the first mass bombing of Tokyo during World War II.

12. Windward valleys receive much less moisture than leeward valleys.

13. When a warm front overtakes a cold front, precipitation is widespread.

14. Sea and land breezes are caused by uneven heating and cooling of land and water.

15. A single bolt of lightning produces as much power as a nuclear power plant for a few seconds.

Completion:

1. _____ is the amount of water vapor in air.

2. When relative humidity reaches 100 percent, the air is _____.

3. Air becomes _____ when it has cooled below its dew point but water remains as vapor.

4. A/an _____ is a visible concentration of water droplets or ice crystals in air.

5. _____ are broad sheet-like clouds.

6. _____ clouds are column-like clouds with flat bottoms and a billowy top.

7. _____ _____ occurs when warm moist air from the sea blows onto cooler land.

8. When air blows against a mountainside, it is forced to rise, by a process called _____ _____.

9. _____ is the horizontal movement of air in response to differences in air pressure.

10. A low-pressure region with its accompanying surface wind is called a/an _____.

11. A high-pressure region with outward spiralling surface wind is called a/an _____.

12. A/an _____ _____ forms when a warm air mass is trapped between two colder air masses.

13. When air currents rise and fall simultaneously within the same cloud, _____ _____ is created.

14. A/an _____ is a small, short-lived, funnel-shaped storm that protrudes from the base of a cumulonimbus cloud.

Answers for Chapter 16

Multiple Choice : 1. c; 2. a; 3. a; 4. b; 5. a; 6. c; 7. d; 8. c; 9. b; 10. c; 11. a; 12. a; 13. b; 14. b; 15. d; 16. b; 17. b; 18. c; 19. c; 20. a

True or False : 1. F; 2. T; 3. T; 4. F; 5. T; 6. T; 7. F; 8. F; 9. T; 10. F; 11. T; 12. F; 13. T; 14. T; 15. T

Completion: 1. Humidity; 2. saturated; 3. supersaturated; 4. cloud; 5. Stratus; 6. Cumulus; 7. Advection fog; 8. orographic lifting; 9. Wind; 10. cyclone; 11. anticyclone; 12. occluded front; 13. wind shear; 14. tornado

CHAPTER 17

Climate

Discussion

Climate and climate change are such important topics in modern Earth Science that we have expanded our coverage of these topics from one Chapter to two. In this chapter, we discuss the mechanisms that regulate planetary climate, climate zones of the Earth, and urban climates. Chapter 18 reviews important aspects of climate change caused both by natural events and by humans.

In our previous discussions of deserts, glaciers, the atmosphere, and weather, we have already introduced many of the factors that create climate such as wind, ocean currents, albedo, and the effects of altitude and latitude. With the scientific foundation firmly in place, we wrap these basic concepts into one coherent package to create an integrated view of Earth's climate.

The first two sections of this chapter outline the mechanisms that produce global winds and precipitation zones. Major climate zones of the Earth are then described according to the Koeppen climate classification system. Urban regions cover a small proportion of the continental land masses, but because so many people live in them, we discuss how urban climates differ from the climate in the surrounding countryside.

Answers to Discussion Questions

1. (a) Wind is slowed by friction as it passes over the land. If a mountain rises high above the surrounding landscape, the air at the upper elevation is less affected by friction and wind speed is generally greater. In addition, temperature differences between mountains and lowlands generate winds, and updrafts form as surface winds are deflected. Finally, very high mountains rise into jet streams, which are the top portion of the Earth's giant convection cells. Mountains affect precipitation because air rising to cross the peaks often cools so much that moisture condenses, as discussed in the text. (b) As explained in Chapters 14, 15 and 17, oceans currents transport large amounts heat from one region of the globe to another. Because temperature differences create wind, heat transport generates winds. Precipitation is regulated by relative humidity and temperature differences; two factors affected by ocean currents.

2. The center of the doldrum area lies in the hottest part of the Earth. Since the Sun shines directly over the Equator only during the spring and autumn equinoxes, the doldrums drift north of the Equator in June and July, and south in December and January. Since seasons repeat

themselves on a yearly basis, there is less year-to-year variation than month to month variation.

3. Airline pilots would expect high altitude winds moving from the southwest.

4. The warm air cools as it ascends and eventually stops rising when it hits the tropopause and is blocked by the warmer air in the stratosphere.

5. If surface water is denser than deep water, it sinks; if it is less dense, it floats. In temperate and tropical oceans, warm surface water lies on top of cold deep water. Now imagine that at given salinities of the layers, the surface water would become denser than the deep water at a temperature of $2\ °C$. If $6°C$ surface water flowed poleward and cooled to $3\ °C$, then little change would occur in the vertical currents because the surface water would still float. However the initial cooling brought the system close to a threshold, because an additional $1\ °C$ cooling would cause the surface water to sink, leading to rapid vertical mixing.

Note that salinity changes have the same effect. If salinity increases through evaporation, surface water can become denser than deep water. Alternatively, if additional fresh water flows into a portion of the ocean where surface water is sinking, then the fresh water could reduce the salinity of the surface water, make it more buoyant, and cause it to stop sinking.

6. (a) Central Oregon which is temperate rainshadow desert or semi-arid prairie, (b) Portland, Oregon which has a marine west coast climate, (c) Amazon basin rainforest which has a humid tropical climate, (d) Sahara desert, a desert formed by subtropical highs, (e) New Orleans which has humid subtropical climate.

Selected Reading

Two general textbooks on climatology are:
A. Henderson-Sellers, *Contemporary Climatology*. New York: Longman Publishing Group, Addison Wesley, 1996.

Russell D. Thompson, *Applied Climatology, Principle and Practice*. New York: Routledge, 1997.

The physics of climatology are discussed in:
Dennis L. Hartman, *Global Physical Climatology*. New York: Academic Press, 1994, 411 pages.

Abraham H. Oort, ed., *Physics of Climate*. American Institute of Physics, 1992, 520 pages.

Two books that discuss climate modelling are:

K. McGuffle, Ann Henderson-Sellers, and Kendal McGuffle, *A Climate Modelling Primer: Research and Development in Climates and Climatology, 2nd ed.* New York: John Wiley, 1997.

Kevin E. Trenberth, ed., *Climate System Modelling.* New York: Cambridge University Press, 1993, 788 pages.

The interaction between climate and weather are explained in
Edward Linacre and Bart Geerts, *Climates and Weather Explained, An Introduction from a Southern Perspective.* New York: Routledge, 1997, 464 pages.

Chapter 17 Test

Multiple Choice:

1. Which of the following statements about climate is correct?
(a) Temperature decreases steadily with increasing longitude. (b) Temperature increases steadily with increasing altitude. (c) All regions at a given latitude have approximately the same temperature. (d) Seasonal temperature changes are more pronounced at high latitudes than at lower latitudes.

2. The three-cell model of global wind circulation shows
(a) three cells of global air flow bordered by three high-pressure regions; (b) three cells of global air flow bordered by three low-pressure regions; (c) three cells of global air flow bordered by alternating bands of high and low pressure; (d) that global wind systems are generated solely by temperature differences between the equator and the poles.

3. The horse latitudes (30 ° north and south latitudes) and the doldrums (approximately 0 ° latitude) are both noted for regular calms, but they differ in that
(a) air in the doldrums is moving vertically downward while air in the horse latitudes is moving vertically upward; (b) rain is frequent in the doldrums while it is much less frequent in the horse latitudes; (c) rain is infrequent in the doldrums while it is more frequent in the horse latitudes; (d) the doldrums is a region of high pressure and the horse latitudes have low pressure.

4. Surface winds moving toward the equator are deflected by the Coriolis force, so they blow from the _____ in the Northern Hemisphere and from the _____ in the Southern Hemisphere.
(a) northeast, southeast; (b) northeast, southwest; (c) northwest, southeast; (d) northwest, southwest.

5. When warm air is heated by the Sun and rises at the equator
(a) it is deflected by the Coriolis force and sinks at the equator in the evening; (b) it travels at high elevation, is deflected by the Coriolis force, and sinks at the poles; (c) it splits and travels poleward, moving due north and south; (d) it splits, travels poleward, is deflected by the Coriolis force, and sinks at 30° North and South latitudes.

6. The polar easterlies and prevailing westerlies converge at approximately
(a) 60° latitude; (b) 60° longitude; (c) 30° latitude; (d) 0° latitude; (e) the poles.

7. In the three-cell model, global wind patterns are generated by
(a) adiabatic expansion; (b) surface ocean currents; (c) the jet stream; (d) heat-driven convection currents that are directed by the Earth's rotation.

8. Which of the following statements about the relationship between deep ocean currents and climate is true?
(a) Because the deep ocean water is not in contact with the atmosphere, deep ocean currents do not affect climate. (b) At times in Earth's history when cool salty water has sunk, the planet has experienced abnormally warm climate. (c) In the past, when the North Atlantic deep current slowed or stopped, the Gulf Stream veered southward resulting in global cooling. (d) In the past, when the North Atlantic current slowed or stopped, the Gulf Stream sped up, causing global warming.

9. The Earth's major climate zones are classified primarily by
(a) temperature and precipitation; (b) latitude and altitude; (c) pressure and wind belts; (d) geographic position; (e) oceans and mountains.

10. The climate zone (or biome) associated with rainfall of 15 centimeters per year is
(a) tropical rainforest; (b) tropical savanna; (c) desert; (d) Mediterranean; (e) marine west coast.

11. The climate zone (or biome) associated with dry summers, rainy winters, and moderate temperature year-round is
(a) tropical rainforest; (b) desert; (c) Mediterranean; (d) marine west coast.

12. The climate zone (or biome) associated with abundant rainfall year round and greater temperature difference between night and day than from June to December is
(a) tropical rainforest; (b) tropical savanna; (c) desert; (d) Mediterranean; (e) marine west coast.

13. Areas that are influenced by warm ocean currents with cool summers, warm winters and abundant precipitation year-round are in the _____ climate zone.
(a) Mediterranean; (b) marine west coast; (c) humid tropical; (d) tropical savanna; (e) none of these.

14. As warm air rises over a city, a local _____ develops, and rainfall is _____ than in the surrounding countryside.

(a) high pressure; greater (b) high pressure; less (c) low pressure; greater (d) low pressure; less.

True or False:

1. Global wind systems are generated only by the temperature difference between the equator and the poles.

2. High-altitude winds from the equator continue to flow all the way to the Poles because they are deflected by the Coriolis effect.

3. Many of the world's great deserts are located in the horse latitudes.

4. The great wheat belts of the United States, Canada, and Russia all lie between 60 ° and 90° north latitude.

5. In regions where warm oceans lie adjacent to cooler land, humid maritime air blows inland, leading to abundant precipitation.

6. A tropical monsoon climate has greater total precipitation and greater monthly variation than tropical savanna.

7. In a Mediterranean climate more than 75 percent of the annual rainfall occurs in summer.

8. Temperate rainforests are common in continental interiors.

9. The climate of cities is measurably different from that of the surrounding rural regions.

10. Storm fronts frequently remain over cities longer than they remain over the surrounding country side.

Completion:

1. Air rises at the convergence of the prevailing westerlies and the polar easterlies, forming a low-pressure boundary zone called the _____ _____.

2. The _____ _____ _____ marks the boundary between cold polar air and the warm, moist westerly flow that originates in the subtropics.

3. The _____ _____ _____ is used by climatologists throughout the world to define principle climate groups.

4. A/an _____ is a community of plants living in a large geographic area characterized by a particular climate.

5. A/an _____ _____ is a tropical region with large seasonal variations in rainfall with a moderate amount of rain that supports grassland with scattered small trees and shrubs.

6. A _____ _____ climate is also tropical with large seasonal variations in rainfall. However, in this region, both the total precipitation and the seasonal variation in precipitation are greater than in question, 7, above.

7. The _____ _____ is characterized by dry summers, rainy winters, and moderate temperature. This climate zone occurs along the coast in southern California.

8. _____ _____ _____ grow in temperate regions where rainfall is greater that 100 centimeters per year (40 in/yr) and is constant throughout the year.

9. The polar biome where trees cannot survive, and low-lying plants such as mosses, grasses, flowers, and a few small bushes cover the land is called _____.

10. The fact that the center of Washington DC is more than 3 ° warmer than outlying areas demonstrates the _____ _____ _____ effect.

Answers for Chapter 17

Multiple Choice: 1. d; 2. c; 3. b; 4. a; 5. d; 6. a; 7. d; 8. c; 9. a; 10. c; 11. d; 12. a; 13. b; 14. c.

True or False: 1. F; 2. F; 3. T; 4. F; 5. T; 6. T; 7. F; 8. F; 9. T; 10. T.

Completion : 1. polar front; 2. polar jet stream; 3. Koeppen climate classification; 4. biome; 5. tropical savanna; 6. tropical monsoon; 7. Mediterranean climate; 8. Temperate rain forests; 9. tundra; 10. urban heat island.

CHAPTER 18

Climate Change

Discussion

Unit VI, **Human Interactions with Earth Systems**, is new to the second edition of Earth Science and the Environment. We built this unit by collecting material that was scattered throughout the first edition and by adding a significant amount of new material. In the first edition, we covered climate change in two sections within a broader chapter on Climate. In recognition of the importance of this topic in modern Earth Science, we have expanded our coverage to an entire chapter.

We start this chapter by documenting that climate has changed repeatedly and often dramatically throughout Earth history. Recent measurements have shown that within the past 100,000 years dramatic temperature shifts have occurred within five to ten years. In contrast, global temperature has been exceptionally stable during recorded history.

The present argument about human impact on climate must be framed within the context of the 4.6 billion year history of natural climate change. During our discussion of industrial carbon dioxide emissions and global warming, we have been careful evaluate the reliability of the data, and to distinguish fact from inference. We also point out that there is not necessarily a linear relationship between the amount of carbon dioxide in the atmosphere and global temperature. We hope to encourage classroom discussion of this important topic.

Answers to Discussion Questions

1. Many examples are possible. The cliche "the straw that broke the camel's back" is a common expression of threshold effects. The assassination of Archduke Francis Ferdinand didn't, by itself, start World War I. The effects of nationalism, imperialism, military expansion, and numerous other crises brought Europe to a political threshold and the Duke's assassination provided "the straw that broke the camels back" to push the continent over the brink. Mechanical mechanisms often fail through feedback sequences. If a balancing weight on the front wheel of your car falls off, the loss of the weight, by itself doesn't affect the front suspension. However, when the wheel wobbles, the tire wobbles and the wobbling tire causes other systems to fail such as wheel bearings and tie rod ends. Personal arguments also commonly escalate through feedback mechanisms.

2. Historical records are valuable only within the range of human writing and painting, which

goes back a few thousand years to as much as a few tens of thousands of years. Pollen records are limited both by the availability of abundant pollen in the fossil record and modern ecosystems to calibrate against. Thus pollen records take us back a few hundred thousand years. Plankton assemblages are well preserved in large scale marine depositional environments, and can be calibrated against modern plankton populations, so this method can be used to measure climates tens of millions of years ago. Beyond that, lack of data (sea floor rocks and sediment are recycled back into the mantle in subduction zones) and difficulties in calibrating plankton abundances with modern systems, limit the usefulness of this system.

3. The surest way reduce carbon dioxide emissions is to reduce the total quantity of fuel burned. This goal can be achieved by social or technical solutions. Social solutions involve altering personal habits, such as carpooling or turning down the thermostat. Technical solutions involve switching to more efficient technologies, such as cars that get better gas milage or more efficient heating and insulation systems. Many analysts argue that moderate reduction of carbon dioxide emissions can be achieved at a profit, due to the fuel saved. However, others disagree and argue that significant carbon dioxide emissions would be so costly that they would cripple the modern global economy. Most experts argue that the answer lies somewhere between these two extremes, but no one knows exactly what the costs will be.

4. Even a small change in global temperature can alter species distribution, rainfall patterns, food productivity, and distribution of disease. Changes in species abundances affect local and global ecosystems, which are environmental concerns. Changes in rainfall affects food production. If a previously fertile area became less fertile and people were to become poor or poorer, established political order could be threatened. Also if the gap between poor and rich nations widens, global political stability could be threatened.

Malaria and many other tropical diseases concentrate in warm climates. If global warming occurs, these disease organisms and vectors will expand their range. For example, malaria mosquitos will migrate to higher latitudes, infecting people who previously lived outside their range.

5. A "yes" answer centers on the need to slow human-induced global warming. "No" answers revolve around the concern that developing countries have not agreed to emissions reductions, so business will shift to these regions. According to this argument, the predicted economic loss to developing countries would be greater than the predicted economic loss from the effects of global warming.

6. The Milankovitch orbital cycles have produced alternate cooling and warming throughout Earth history. Yet ice ages have not advanced and retreated continuously. Gould's quote states

that other, unrelated factors, have caused the Earth to be so warm during most of Earth history that even the coldest part of the Milankovitch cycle has not produced glaciation.

7. Rapid plate motion occurs when sea floor spreading is rapid. The resultant high volume mid-oceanic ridge raises sea level and lowers weathering of coastal limestone. Increased volcanic activity releases large quantities of carbon dioxide into the air. These events tend to cause global warming.

However, many mountains are composed of limestone. When the limestone is exposed, weathering increases. In addition, if organic rich sediment is submerged where it doesn't decay, terrestrial carbon is stored. These processes remove carbon from the atmosphere and lead to global cooling.

Without more data, it would be impossible to predict whether global temperatures rose or fell. In the example cited here, David des Marais predicted global cooling.

Selected Reading

The history of climate and the effects of pollutants on global climate change are assessed in: Francesca Lyman, Irving Mintzer, Kathleen Courrier, and James MacKenzie, *The Greenhouse Trap: What We are Doing to the Atmosphere and How We Can Slow Global Warming*. Boston: Beacon Press, 1990. 190 pages.

Stephen H. Schneider, *Laboratory Earth: The Planetary Gamble We Can't Afford to Lose*. New York: Basic Books, 1997, 174 pages.

Kenneth M. Strzepek and Joel B. Smith, eds., *As Climate Changes*. New York: Cambridge University Press, 1995, 240 pages.

Four books on global warming are:
W. Neil Adger and Katrina Brown, *Land Use and the Causes of Global Warning*. New York: John Wiley and Sons, 1994, 271 pages.

Ross Gelbspan, *The Heat is On: The High Stakes Battle Over Earth's Threatened Climate*. New York: Addison-Wesley, 1997, 278 pages.
John Houghton, *Global Warming: The Complete Briefing*. Oxford: Lion Publishing, 1994, 192 pages;

Michael L. Parsons, *Global Warming: The Truth Behind the Myth*. New York: Plenum, 1995,

271 pages.

A classic paper on advances and retreats of the Pleistocene glaciers, and a modern sequel are:
J. D. Hays, John Imbrie, and N. J. Shackleton, "Variations in the Earth's Orbit: Pacemaker of the Ice Ages." *Science, 194*:(1121), 1976.

Wallace S. Broecker and George H. Denton, "What Drives Glacial Cycles?" *Scientific American, 1*: 49-56, 1990.

For a historical look at climate change:
L. A. Frakes, J. E. Francis, and J. I. Syktus, *Climate Modes of the Phanerozoic*, New York: Cambridge University Press, 1992.

Elisabeth S. Vrba, George H. Denton, Timothy C. Partridge, and Lloyd H. Burckle, *Paleoclimate and Evolution, With emphasis on Human Origins*. New Haven, CT: Yale University Press, 1995, 547 pages.

Several journal articles used to prepare this chapter are:
Gerard Bond, et al., "Correlations Between Climate Records from North Atlantic Sediments and Greenland Ice." *Nature, 365*(143), September 9, 1993

Robert J. Charlson and Tom M. L. Wigley, "Sulfate Aerosol and Climate Change." *Scientific American*, February 1994

R. J. Charlson, S. E. Schwartz, J. M. Hales, R. D. Cess, J. A. Coakley, Jr., J. E. Hansen, and D. J. Hofmann, "Climate Forcing by Anthropogenic Aerosols." *Science, 225*:423, 1992.

Greenland Ice-core Project Members, "Climate Instability During the Last Interglacial Period Recorded in the GRIP Ice Core." *Nature, 364*(203), July 15, 1993.

David Hanson, "Record Low Ozone Levels Observed Over Antarctica." *Chemical and Engineering News*, April 10, 1995.

Bette Hileman, "Climate Observations Substantiate Global Warming Models." *Chemical and Engineering News*, November 27, 1995.
J. T. Kiehl and B. P. Briegleb; "The Relative Role of Sulfate Aerosols and Greenhouse Gases in Climate Forcing." *Science, 260*(311), April 16, 1993.

166

Alan Newman, "Ozone Hole Effects Documented in UN Report." *Environmental Science and Technology, 29*(2), 1995.

Edward A. Parson and Owen Greene, "The Complex Chemistry of the International Ozone Agreements." *Environment,37*(2), March 1995.

Wilfred M. Post, et al., "The Global Carbon Cycle." *American Scientist, 78* July-August 1990.

Chapter 18 Test

Multiple Choice:

1. Which of the following statements about climate change is true?
(a) The Earth's mean global temperature was relatively constant before the Industrial Revolution.
(b) The Earth's mean global temperature has increased steadily throughout geologic time. (c) The Earth's mean global temperature has decreased steadily throughout geologic time. (d) The Earth's mean global temperature has fluctuated throughout geologic time.

2. If sea level rose, the global albedo would _____; influencing a _____ in global temperature.
(a) increase, increase; (b) increase, decrease; (c) decrease, increase; (d) decrease, decrease.

3. Oxygen isotope ratios in Greenland and Antarctic glaciers
(a) reflect sea surface temperatures 500 million to one billion years ago; (b) are the most useful method for determining global temperatures in the past 100 years; (c) directly measure the temperature of the ocean depths 10,000 years ago; (d) reflect sea surface temperatures within the past 110,000 years; (e) reflect sea surface temperatures within the past 35 million years.

4. The most useful of the methods listed below for determining paleotemperatures one billion years ago is
(a) studying ancient tillites and laterites; (b) measuring oxygen isotope ratios in Greenland ice; (c) studying terminal moraines; (d) counting tree rings.

5. Which of the following is not true for carbon dioxide? It
(a) dissolves in seawater; (b) absorbs infrared radiation; (c) reacts with other chemicals to form solid rocks; (d) is destroyed when organic matter is burned.

6. During photosynthesis
(a) carbon dioxide, which is a greenhouse gas, is released; (b) oxygen, which is not a greenhouse gas, is released; (c) carbon dioxide, which is not a greenhouse gas, is released; (d) oxygen, which is a greenhouse gas, is released.

7. Marine corals and shelled organisms
(a) release carbon dioxide into the atmosphere as they convert carbonate ions to hard shells; (b) convert carbon from the remains of dead plants and animals to hard shells; (c) absorb calcium and carbonate ions from seawater and convert them to hard shells; (d) extract carbon from the lower crust and upper mantle.

8. Global atmospheric carbon dioxide has _____ during the last 120 years.
(a) remained the same; (b) increased; (c) decreased; (d) oscillated dramatically.

9. About 55 million years ago climate warmed. Surface water evaporated and the salinity of sea water _____. This water _____ and _____ methyl hydrates on the sea floor, leading to a/an _____ in global temperature.
(a) decreased, floated on the surface, melted, increase; (b) decreased, sank, melted increase; (c) increased, sank, melted, increase; (d) increased, sank, froze, decrease.

10. Which of the following is not a greenhouse gas?
(a) nitrogen (b) carbon dioxide (c) methane (d) chlorofluorocarbons

11. The atmosphere has warmed by about _____ during the last century.
(a) 0.5°C; (b) 5°C; (c) .15°C; (d) 1.5°C; (e) 15°C.

12. Which of the following changes in energy policy would reduce emission of greenhouse gases?
(a) Switch from high sulfur coal to low sulfur coal. (b) Switch from gasoline to coal. (c) Switch from coal to gasoline. (d) Switch from coal to natural gas. (e) Switch from coal to nuclear fuels.

13. According to one argument, if the atmosphere warmed, the Gulf Stream would be altered and global climate would cool. Which of the following mechanisms is used to support this argument? The surface of the ocean would become warmer and
(a) more buoyant; it would stop sinking and shut off the vertical current, deflecting the Gulf Stream; (b) denser; it would sink, increasing the vertical current, deflecting the Gulf Stream; (c) more buoyant; it would stop sinking and shut off the vertical current, causing the Gulf Stream to speed up; (d) denser; it would sink, increasing the vertical current, causing the Gulf Stream to speed up.

14. Rapid plate movement and sea-floor spreading cause global _____ because the mid-oceanic ridges become _____.
(a) sea-level rise, wider; (b) sea-level fall, thinner; (c) sea-level fall, wider; (d) sea-level rise, thinner.

15. The Mount Pinatubo eruption
(a) warmed the atmosphere by releasing carbon dioxide; (b) cooled the atmosphere by releasing carbon dioxide; (c) warmed the atmosphere by releasing ash and sulfur compounds; (d) cooled the atmosphere by releasing ash and sulfur compounds.

16. Changes in the Earth's orbit around the Sun
(a) cannot cause climate change; (b) cause climate change only when the continents are near the Poles; (c) may cause climate by altering the frequency of sunspots; (d) cause climate change by altering the frequency and intensity of tides; (e) may have caused the advances and retreats of the Pleistocene glaciers.

17. A meteorite impact would
(a) cool the atmosphere by releasing carbon dioxide; (b) warm the atmosphere by releasing radioactive iridium; (c) cool the atmosphere by releasing dust and gas; (d) warm the atmosphere by releasing carbon dioxide.

True or False:

1. Scientists study old landscape paintings to chronicle historical climates.

2. ^{18}O is the most abundant isotope of oxygen.

3. If you discovered a lithified coral reef on a glaciated mountain, you could deduce that mean global temperature was warmer at the time the reef was deposited than it is today.

4. The $^{18}O/^{16}O$ ratio in glacial ice measures the rate of flow of ocean currents in the past.

5. If there were no atmosphere, the Earth would be frigidly cold at night.

6. When carbon dioxide gas dissolves in sea water, it forms limestone.

7. Carbon is abundant in the biosphere because it is the primary constituent of bones, exoskeletons, and the shells of corals and other reef-building organisms.

8. Weathering of carbonate rocks removes carbon dioxide from the atmosphere and cools the Earth.

9. Carbon dioxide is released into the atmosphere during volcanic eruptions.

10. Scientists calculate that if global temperature increases rainfall in the Great Plains in North America would increase but soil moisture would decrease.

11. Solar output has fluctuated by about 2 percent during the past few thousand years.

12. In about 5 billion years the Sun's hydrogen fuel will run out, the Sun will shut down, and the Earth will freeze.

Completion:

1. Scientists determine past tree species abundances by studying _____ preserved in lake bottoms and bogs.

2. _____ is a sedimentary rock formed from glacial debris.

3. Carbon exists in the atmosphere mostly as _____ and _____ _____.

4. When carbon dioxide gas dissolves in sea water, it reacts to form _____ and _____ ions.

5. Marine organisms absorb calcium and carbonate ions from seawater and convert them to _____ _____ in shells and other hard body parts.

6. When coal burns, carbon is released into the atmosphere as _____ _____.

7. When methane reacts under pressure on the ocean floor it forms _____ _____.

8. The four industrial greenhouse gases are _____, _____, _____, and _____ _____.

9. _____ is the measure of the reflectivity of a surface.

10. Solar magnetic storms produce _____ which may affect climate on Earth.

Answers for Chapter 18

Multiple Choice: 1. d; 2. c; 3. d; 4. a; 5. d; 6. b; 7. c; 8. c; 9. c; 10. a; 11. a; 12. e; 13. a; 14. a; 15. d; 16. e; 17. c.

True of False: 1. T; 2. F; 3. F; 4. F; 5. T; 6. F; 7. F; 8. T; 9. T; 10. T; 11. F; 12. F.

Completion: 1. pollen; 2. Tillite; 3. carbon dioxide and methane; 4. bicarbonate, carbonate; 5. calcium carbonate; 6. carbon dioxide; 7. methyl hydrate; 8. carbon dioxide, methane, chlorofluorocarbons, nitrous oxides; 9. Albedo; 10. sunspots.

CHAPTER 19

Air Pollution

Discussion

This chapter introduces the major sources of air pollutants and their health effects on humans. Two atmospheric mechanisms exacerbate air pollution: secondary chemical reactions that produce smog and acid precipitation, and meteorological conditions that concentrate pollutants in inversion layers.

In recent years, both scientists and non-scientists have become increasingly involved in public policy decisions regarding pollution control. Two major questions are: how much does pollution control cost, and how much control are we willing to pay for? Engineers can tell us how much it costs to place abatement devices on existing equipment such as catalytic converters on automobiles or scrubbers on coal fired power plants. But recently people have begun to realize that such remedial solutions may not be the most effective and that pollution can be reduced more economically by re-evaluating fundamental procedures. Thus if gasoline powered automobiles are too polluting, perhaps commuters could use electric cars or more mass transit. Conservation of electricity is a more effective and cheaper way to reduce air pollution from power plants than is the addition of pollution abatement equipment. Advocates of nuclear power claim that the health effects from operating nuclear generators and disposing of their wastes are less than those from burning coal. The information in this chapter will broaden students background for these important discussions.

In the 1970s, Paul Crutzen, Sherwood Rowland, and Mario Molina showed that some industrial pollutants and naturally occurring compounds drift into the stratosphere and destroy ozone. In 1995, Crutzen, Rowland, and Molina won the Nobel prize in chemistry for their work on the ozone hole. Critics argued that their work was applied, not basic research and was therefore not worthy of the prize. However, the Nobel committee wrote that "the three researchers contributed to our salvation from a global environmental problem that could have had catastrophic consequences."

Answers to Discussion Questions

1. (a) Particulate; (b) gaseous; (c) none; (d) and (e) gaseous and particulate.

2. When the pollutants finally reach the ground, they have become more diluted, hence, less harmful. Some studies indicate that if the concentration is diluted below a threshold level, some

potentially harmful pollutants may become benign. However, certain effects, such as an increase in the carbon dioxide level or acid rain, cannot be prevented by chimneys.

3. Figure 19-5 shows that temperature decreasing continuously with altitude is most conducive to rapid dispersal of pollutants. The least favorable conditions occur under an inversion layer, as shown in Figure 19-6.

4. Method (a) is uncertain because many factors change with time. For example, the age-sex distribution of a population changes and the quality of medical care changes. However, if a factory moves into an area, and a few years later an otherwise rare disease affects an abnormally large percentage of the population, than one might suspect that the pollution emitted by that factory could be a cause. Method (b & d) can be effective for studies of diseases with immediate onset, such as severe asthma attacks or respiratory congestion. However, they are useless for epidemiological studies of diseases such as cancer and birth defects that appear years or decades after exposure. Method (c) has limited usefulness unless the level of industrial activity and the release of pollutants changes with the seasons and natural seasonal disease fluctuations can be statistically eliminated. Method (e) is commonly used in epidemiological studies. If people in a polluted area have a higher incidence of certain diseases than people in a demographically similar population who live in a low air pollution area, than the pollution becomes suspect.

5. Air quality standards do not apply to the concentrations at the stack. Therefore, you would need to know what the emission standards were for the plant in question, to determine whether there was a violation. Alternatively, you could analyze air near the plant at ground level, and then you could use the ambient standards as a guide, but you would have to prove that the plant in question is the source. A final possibility would be to calculate the dilution expected between the stack and the ground level, and apply this factor to the stack concentration to predict the expected ambient ground level concentration. Such calculations are carried out by meteorologists, who use mathematical models that have been tested experimentally.

6. Oxidation of sulfur to sulfur dioxide in the flame; further oxidation to sulfuric acid in the atmosphere as described in the text.

7. Oxides of nitrogen.

8. The environmental benefits because trash is used as a fuel, conserving fossil fuel supplies and reducing solid waste disposal problems. The question of drawbacks is difficult because we don't know the health effects of the very small doses of pollutants that escape from incinerators with state of the art pollution control. Citizens groups also argue that pollution control devices can

break, and therefore there is a risk of high emissions of toxic substances for short periods of time. Industry argues that these risks are small compared with other risks that people normally accept, such as fatal mechanical failures in automobiles or airplanes.

Selected Reading

Five background references for this chapter are:
J. Clarence Davies and Jan Mazurek, *Pollution Control in the United States: Evaluating the System*. Washington DC: Resources For the Future books, 1998, 336 pages.

Derek Elsom, *Smog Alert, Managing Urban Air Quality*. Covelo, CA: Earthscan, 1996, 192 pages.

Thad Godish, *Air Quality, 2nd ed*. Boca Raton, FL: Lewis Publishers, 1997, 512 pages.

Lawrence H. Keith and Mary M. Walker, *Handbook of Air Toxics*. Boca Raton, FL: Lewis Publishers, 1995, 640 pages.

William Vatavuk, *Estimating the Costs of Air Pollution Control*. Chelsea, MI: Lewis Publishers, 1990, 235 pages.

The effect of air pollution on vegetation is discussed in:
James J. MacKenzie and Mohamed T. El-Ashry, *Air Pollution's Toll on Forests and Crops*. New Haven, CT: Yale University Press, 1990, 384 pages.

Kullervo Kuusela, *Forest Resources in Europe, 1950-1990*. New York: Cambridge University Press, 1995, 154 pages.

Mohammad Yunus and Muhammad Iqbal, eds., *Plant Response to Air Pollution*. New York: John Wiley, 1996, 558 pages.

Chapter 19 Test

Multiple Choice:

1. If pure coal burned completely, it would produce
(a) benzene and toxic volatiles; (b) carbon dioxide and water; (c) carbon dioxide; soot, and fly ash; (d) oxygen and water.

2. The primary source of nitrogen oxide pollution is
(a) automobile exhaust; (b) coal fired power plants; (c) nuclear power plants; (d) chemical manufacturing.

3. An aerosol is
(a) any small particle larger than a molecule and suspended in air; (b) any air pollutant; (c) any toxic air pollutant; (d) an air pollutant composed of gaseous molecules.

4. Two examples of air pollutants that are not released directly into the air by any industrial process, but are generated by reactions within the atmosphere are
(a) acid precipitation and fly ash; (b) acid precipitation and smog; (c) smog and fly ash; (d) benzene and fly ash; (e) nitrogen oxides and carbon monoxide.

5. Fly ash is
(a) released mainly from automobile exhaust; (b) a precursor to acid rain; (c) a precursor to photochemical smog; (d) mineral matter released when coal is burned.

6. Under normal conditions, the air at higher elevations is _____ than he air near the ground. As a result, _____
(a) cooler, air pollutants remain near the ground; (b) cooler, air pollutants rise and are diluted; (c) warmer, air pollutants remain near the ground; (d) warmer, air pollutants rise and are diluted.

7. During an inversion, the air at higher elevations is _____ than the air near the ground. As a result, _____
(a) cooler, air pollutants remain near the ground; (b) cooler, air pollutants rise and are diluted; (c) warmer, air pollutants remain near the ground; (d) warmer, air pollutants rise and are diluted.

8. An example of an epidemiological study is:
(a) Health records of workers in a chemical plant are compared with those of farmers living in the surrounding countryside. (b) Rats are fed high doses of an air pollutant and tested to see how many contract cancer. (c) Air pollutants are mixed in an experimental room which is lit up by sunlamps. (d) Atmospheric temperature is recorded as a function of altitude and the temperature profile is compared with the concentration of pollutants.

9. Acidic precipitation is produced
(a) when sulfur dioxide and oxides of nitrogen dissolve in water droplets in the atmosphere; (b) whenever fuels are burned; (d) by nuclear fission reactors; (d) by atmospheric inversion; (e) when sunlight reacts with automobile exhaust.

10. The major source of sulfur dioxide pollution is
(a) automobile exhaust; (b) coal-fired electric generators; (c) home furnaces; (d) evaporation of paints and pesticides; (e) nuclear power plants.

11. In the United States the cost of deterioration of buildings and materials from acid precipitation
(a) is a minor problem; (b) is estimated at several billion dollars per year; (c) is estimated at several million dollars per year; (d) was high a decade ago but is now minimal due to implementation of the Clean Air Act.

12. Photochemical smog can be produced artificially by a combination of
(a) automobile exhaust and UV lamps; (b) UV lamps and ozone; (c) gasoline vapor and oxygen; (d) gasoline vapor and UV lamps.

13. Which of the following statements about dioxin is true?
(a) Large amounts of dioxin are manufactured in the United States; (b) Scientists have proven that vary small doses of dioxin in the environment are carcinogenic; (c) Dioxin concentrates and accumulates in human muscle tissue; (d) Most scientists agree that exposure to high concentrations of dioxin causes cancer.

14. Solar energy breaks oxygen molecules apart in the stratosphere, releasing _____ which combine with additional oxygen molecules to form _____.
(a) oxygen atoms, ozone; (b) ozone, CFCs; (c) ozone, oxygen atoms; (d) oxygen atoms, carbon dioxide.

15. Chlorofluorocarbons
(a) are toxic to humans; (b) combine with dust particles to form aerosols that cool the Earth; (c) react to form ozone; (d) react to destroy ozone.

True or False:

1. Twenty people died from the effects of air pollution in Donora, Pennsylvania in 1948.

2. Even if each factory, power plant, and automobile complies with the Clean Air Act, if the total pollution level exceeds National Ambient Air Quality Standards, then the EPA must set stricter controls.

3. High sulfur dioxide concentrations have been associated with major air pollution disasters of the type that occurred in Donora.

4. Benzene, a product of incomplete combustion of fossil fuels, is a carcinogen.

5. Fly ash is a gaseous air pollutant released when coal is burned.

6. During an atmospheric inversion, upper air is cooler than air near the ground.

7. Ozone is both a pollutant and a beneficial component of the atmosphere, depending on elevation.

8. Epidemiological studies of cigarette smoke are reliable because there is a clear-cut distinction between people who smoke and those who do not.

9. Acid precipitation forms when sulfur dioxide reacts with ozone in the stratosphere.

10. Incompletely burned gasoline in automobile exhaust reacts to deplete ozone in the troposphere.

Completion:

1. The major legislation that dictates Federal air pollution policy is the _____ _____ _____.

2. Today the primary global source of sulfur dioxide pollution is _____ _____ _____.

3. _____ are compounds composed of carbon and hydrogen.

4. A/an _____ compound is one that evaporates readily and therefore easily escapes into the atmosphere.

5. Gases and particulates released during combustion and manufacturing are called _____ _____ _____.

6. Smog is produced when automobile exhaust is exposed to _____.

7. When coal burns, some of minerals escape from the chimney as _____ _____ which settles out as gritty dust.

8. _____ in the stratosphere absorbs ultraviolet radiation.

9. _____ _____ and _____ _____ react in moist air to produce sulfuric acid.

10. _____ is the study of the distribution and determination of health and its disorders.

11. Tree death in West Germany has been attributed to _____ _____.

12. The ozone hole is a condition where the ozone concentration is depleted in the upper layer of the atmosphere known as the _____.

Answers for Chapter 19

Multiple Choice: 1. b; 2. a; 3. a; 4. b; 5. d; 6. b; 7. c; 8. a; 9. a; 10. b; 11. b; 12. a; 13. d; 14. a; 15. d.

True or False: 1. T; 2. T; 3. T; 4. T; 5. F; 6. F; 7. T; 8. T; 9. F; 10. F.

Completion: 1. Clean Air Act; 2. coal-fired electric generators; 3. Hydrocarbons; 4. volatile; 5. primary air pollutants; 6. sunlight; 7. fly ash; 8. Ozone; 9. Sulfur dioxide, sulfur trioxide; 10. Epidemiology; 11. acid precipitation (rain); 12. stratosphere.

CHAPTER 20

Water Resources

Discussion

Over the past few decades, the number of professional jobs in mining and oil exploration has declined, whereas employment in waste disposal, ground-water and stream hydrology, and water pollution problems has increased dramatically. As people have recognized the threats from pollution of soil, ground water, and surface water, they have searched for remedies, and Earth scientists have been at the vanguard of these studies.

Chapter 20 deals with the supply, demand, and use of water, particularly in the United States. Case studies comprise a large part of this chapter; we feel that they illustrate the utility and environmental impacts of dams, ground water pumping, irrigation, and other forms of water diversion much more clearly than abstract discussions.

The chapter begins by explaining that although 3 times as much water falls on the U.S. as we use, precipitation is not distributed evenly. Some of the driest regions of the U.S. use the greatest amounts of water. Some of our most productive farmland lies in the desert and near-desert regions of the American West - California, Texas, Arizona, and nearby states. These farms are watered by extremely expensive, usually publicly funded irrigation systems. At the same time, farmers in southeastern states, where rainfall is abundant and irrigation often unnecessary, are subsidized not to grow the same crops that are raised and watered by federal irrigation systems in the West.

We then discuss water diversion projects - dams and ground water extraction - and their environmental impacts. This discussion is illustrated with examples from the Ogallala Aquifer, the Columbia River dam complex, the Aswan Dam in Egypt, The 1976 Teton Dam disaster in eastern Idaho, the use of Colorado River water, and the Los Angeles Water Project and its impacts on the Owens Valley. The chapter describes the role of water in international politics - an important factor in the Middle East and other dry, overpopulated parts of the Earth.

We then describe pollution, risk assessment, cost-benefit analysis, and remediation of ground- and surface water pollution, with examples chosen from the Love Canal disaster, the Yucca Mountain Nuclear Waste Repository, the Cuyahoga River fire, the Great Lakes, and the Butte, Montana Superfund site (the largest one in the United States).

Answers to Discussion Questions

1. (a) If global temperature rose, more water would evaporate from the oceans and therefore

precipitation on the continents would increase. However, as discussed in Chapter 18, in a hotter world evaporation might be more rapid. The effects on surface and ground water reserves are uncertain. If, as expected, precipitation fell in extreme events, stream flow might exhibit higher highs and lower lows. The answer to this questions reminds us once again that Earth systems are complex and do not always respond to changes in a straightforward manner. Climatologists also calculate that global warming might lead to changes in wind and current patterns. These changes might alter the distribution of precipitation over the U.S. On a global scale, monsoon cycles in Asia and jet streams in higher latitudes might change. If so, rainfall patterns would change, humid areas might be desertified, deserts could receive more rainfall. These changes could affect global distribution of surface and ground-water reserves, and might change agriculture and the economy of many areas. A rise in temperature might also lead a rise in sea level. The effect of melting of coastal glaciers could be offset if increased precipitation led to an increase in the amount of permanent ice on continents. The situation is further complicated by the fact that the climate in some areas in Northern Canada and the USSR is cold enough for glaciation if more moisture were available. Therefore, paradoxically, a warming trend could initiate glaciation in some places.

(b) If global temperature fell, less water would evaporate from the oceans and therefore precipitation and runoff on the continents would decrease. Semiarid lands could be desertified. The distribution precipitation might change, with unknown consequences. Ice would be retained longer and in some areas glaciers would expand.

2. Surface water diversion projects usually involve construction of dams and aqueducts. The benefits of surface water systems arise from the fact that they store water otherwise lost during high runoff such as in the spring, for use during the dry summer months. Dams can also be constructed to include electrical generators, and thus, surface diversion systems serve a dual purpose.

Drawbacks of dam-aqueduct systems are many. They are extremely expensive to build, so expensive that no major dam has ever been built in the U.S. without federal and/or state funding. As a result, taxpayers foot the bills, but commonly only a few industries and agribusiness corporations receive the heavily subsidized benefits. Dams and aqueduct systems also generate environmental hazards and degradation of many kinds, as documented in the chapter.

Ground water diversion systems have the advantage of tapping reservoirs that, on a global average, contain 30 times more water than all surface water combined. In addition, it is inexpensive to pump ground water relative to costs of dam and aqueduct construction. Ground water is more widespread than large surface water sources, so it commonly can be obtained locally. Thus large aqueduct systems to carry it long distances are not needed. It is normally clean, and requires no treatment before use. The main drawback of pumping ground water is that in some very important aquifers such as Ogallala, the rate of recharge of the aquifer is orders of magnitude slower than current extraction rates. The water is, as a result, non-renewable. In the U.S. a major part of our agricultural productivity depends on this vanishing water source. Excessive pumping also causes subsidence and resultant damage to surface structures, and in coastal areas can cause salt water intrusion.

3. An answer to any question regarding motives (WHY do we build dams?) probably reflects the bias of the person offering the answer rather than the real reasons behind dam-building. Answers to this question may include: we need dams to provide water and electricity for agriculture (in the U.S. food is cheaper relative to wages than it is in most other nations); we need them for industry, we need them for home consumption; senators and congressmen spent taxpayers money on dams in their own states and districts in order to "buy" votes from local consumers of cheap, subsidized water and electricity; the Bureau of Reclamation and U.S. Army Corps of Engineers must continue to build dams and other diversion projects to justify their own existences and salaries.

This question is more likely to provoke a lively debate than to provide any "real" answers regarding motives.

4. The long-term scenarios are many, but fall into two general categories: either the region develops new, outside sources of water, or it dries up. The short-term scenarios are equally numerous, and have to do mainly with who continues to get enough water to continue farming and ranching as the water supply diminishes, and who doesn't. What then happens to the land that goes out of production? A recent paper in "Geology" suggests that parts of this region were dry enough to sustain great fields of blowing sand within the past few thousand years, and that the current rainfall is just above the threshold for a return to those conditions (R.F. Madole, 1994, Geology v. 22 no. 6 pp 483-486). This story provides additional material for speculation, particularly when combined with possible decline of soil moisture in the continental interior as a result of global warming.

5. The data given in the chapter provide a framework for discussing how conservation in the three categories of water use can affect total water availability in the U.S. Domestic use accounts for only 10 percent of all water use. Thus, personal and domestic conservation cannot significantly increase total water availability on a large scale. Installation of a low-flow shower head or a water-efficient toilet saves little money at current water rates, and has only a small effect on the total U.S. water budget. Of course, such measures can become important locally because drinking water reserves don't always reflect the total water available. Thus home conservation can become significant if local drinking water reservoirs are inadequate to meet supply and if domestic consumption accounts for a much larger proportion of water use than the national average.

The data make it clear that industry (49 percent) and agriculture (41 percent) are the major water users, and consequently, conservation in these categories is necessary to have a significant effect on the national water budget. Conservation methods available to industry and agriculture are discussed in the text. It is worth stressing that one of the most important water conservation measures available on a national scale is to shift agricultural priorities so that crops requiring a great deal of water are grown in regions of high rainfall, and only crops requiring little water are grown where water is scarce. It makes little sense to grow cotton and rice in the desert, and subsidize farmers in wet regions not to grow the same crops. Only federal subsidies make this situation possible.

6. This is another question dealing with motives (Why?). Again, the answers will reflect the biases of the individual participants in the discussion. It is relevant to the discussion that agriculture in California is heavily subsidized by federal and state support of the irrigation systems, and agriculture in the southeast and south central part of the U.S. is also supported by subsidies. Thus, farmers are working the subsidy system in addition to working the land. The problems seem to lie in a lack of rationale and common sense in our federal agricultural policy.

7. Reasons for the transformation of the American west from a sparsely-settled arid to semi-arid desert to a region with booming cities and intensive agriculture are discussed at length in the chapter. Generally, they have to do with two factors: availability of cheap, heavily-subsidized water, and the fact that much of the Great American Desert is a nice place to live if water is available. Reisner's argument that the current population and economy are unsustainable is supported by the fact that water is being removed from western aquifers faster than the rate of recharge, so it is inevitable that ground water resources will be depleted. Since not enough water flows in surface streams to maintain existing levels of irrigation, failure of the agricultural system is inevitable. Furthermore, soil salinity increases when fields are irrigated year after year and this problem is not easily reversed. A counter argument is that we have technology not available to the ancients. Drainage systems can be built and salt-resistant crops can be genetically engineered. Water could be diverted from British Columbia, where there is an excess. However, such projects are expensive and consume large amounts of energy. Other technological solutions would be to develop and use drought-resistant strains of grain, or to use water more efficiently with advanced irrigation techniques. It is unlikely to imagine that large cities such as Phoenix and Las vegas would become ghost towns. Perhaps agriculture would decline and these cities would rely on high tech industries for their economic base.

8. These cities are situated in localities with a pleasant climate and favorable living conditions except for the lack of water. When federal and state agencies construct water systems to supply the areas, people naturally flock to them to take advantage of the environment. In the case of Las

Vegas, legal gambling created jobs, which also drew people to the city.

9. For: Why let valuable fresh water flow into the ocean when it can be used to increase productivity and augment the economy?
Against: As discussed above, water diversions are expensive and consume energy. Also the issue of buying water from Canada would ultimately place the western water budget dependent on a resource from another country. Such dependence can be beneficial as our petroleum dependence has been, but it is vulnerable to disruption if the political climate changes. In addition, such diversion would cause numerous ecological problems at the source of diversion.

10. The role of water in international relations is discussed in Section 20.4. The part that water plays in relations between Mexico and the U.S. is discussed in the case study of the Colorado River. Water has been a source both of cooperation and of low-level bickering between Canada and the U.S. for many years because the two nations share many rivers and lakes that lie along the border. It would be an interesting exercise for students at colleges and universities near the border to choose a nearby stream or lake shared by the two nations, and research the history of international interactions dealing with that particular waterway.

11.   Sewage: point source
        Disease Organisms: point source
        Plant nutrients: non-point source (agricultural fertilizers) and point source (sewage treatment facilities).
        Industrial organic compounds: point source (factories), non-point source (agricultural pesticides and herbicides)
        Toxic inorganic compounds and metals: point source (mines, factories) and non-point source (road salt)
        Sediment: non-point source (agriculture, logging, road building), point source (mine wastes)
        Radioactive materials: point source
        Heat: point source.

12. Increasing numbers of people in the United States are turning to bottled drinking water in preference to urban, suburban, and even rural public water supplies. The reasons for this trend are numerous, and include mistrust of public officials, mistrust of drinking water standards, and knowledge that some public water supplies are of marginal or worse quality. Other people turn to bottled water sources via the "better safe than sorry" doctrine. A careful person would decide whether or not to use public drinking water sources on the basis of awareness and understanding of drinking water standards and reliable and frequently updated analyses of the water source.

13. Pro: Disposal in injection wells removes toxic waste from storage sites that may be more vulnerable to breaching than deep aquifer storage. In some aquifers, deep well disposal may reliably isolate toxic waste from the environment for thousands of years or more. Deep aquifer storage may be cheaper and would produce less air pollution than incineration or chemical destruction of the wastes. There are many deep storage sites, and a large quantity of toxic material can be disposed of in this way.

Con: Water in deep aquifer toxic waste storage sites may eventually mix with shallow aquifers used by humans. Earthquakes and other tectonic events can result in sudden mixing of a deep aquifer with a shallow one, or the surface environment. If the wastes are non-degradable, they will persist for geologic time, and might eventually return to the surface. If shallow aquifers are pumped dry, humans may eventually need water in the deep aquifers that are now used for toxic waste storage.

Selected Reading

Several books explore the issues of surface water pollution and the Clean Water Act:
Robert W. Adler, Jessica C. Landman, and Diane M. Cameron, *The Clean Water Act 20 Years Later*. Washington, D.C.: Island Press, 1993, 320 pages.

C. Dale Becker and Duane A. Neitzel, eds., *Water Quality in North American River Systems*. Columbus, Ohio: Battelle Press, 1992, 304 pages.

C. F. Mason, *Biology of Freshwater Pollution*, 2nd edition. New York: John Wiley, 1991, 364 pages.

Helen Ingram, *Water Politics: Continuity and Change*. Tucson: University of Arizona, 1990. 158 pages.

Toxic wastes and the Superfund Law are discussed in:
M. Arnoud, M. Barres, and B. Come, *Geology and the Confinement of Toxic Wastes*. Rotterdam, Netherlands: A.A. Balkema, 1993, 610 pages.

Mark H. Dorfman, Warren R. Muir, and Catherine G. Miller, *Environmental Dividends: Cutting More Chemical Wastes*. New York: INFORM, 1992, 272 pages.

Warren Freedman, *Hazardous Waste Liability*. Washington D.C: BNA Books, 1992, 800 pages.

Fred Setterberg and Lonny Shavelson *Toxic Nation: The Fight to Save Our Communities from Chemical Contamination.* New York: Wiley, 1993, 301 pages.

Pollution of ground water and its consequences are discussed in:
Domy C. Adriano, Alex K. Iskandar, and Ishwar P. Murarka, eds., *Contamination of Groundwaters*. Delray Beach, FL: St. Lucie Press, 1994, 536 pages.

Jack E Barbash and Elizabeth A. Resek, *Pesticides in Ground Water: Distributions, Trends, and Governing Factors*. Chelsea,MI: Ann Arbor Press, 1996, 600 pages.

An overview of the nuclear waste problem is given in two documents:
Nicholas Lenssen: *Nuclear Waste: The Problem That Won't Go Away*, Paper 106. Washington, Worldwatch Press, 1991, 62 pp.

Douglas Easterling and Howard Kunreuther, *The Dilemma of Siting a High Level Nuclear Waste Repository*. Norwell, MA, 1995, 286 pages.

Chapter 20 Test

Multiple Choice:

1. In which of the following cases is water both withdrawn and consumed?
(a) You wash your car with water that is pumped from a local well, and the water runs into a storm drain; (b) On a hot sunny day, a farmer uses a sprinkler irrigation system to water his crops; (c) You shower with water taken from a local well, and the water drains into a septic tank near your house; (d) firemen douse a fire by pumping water from a lake.

2. Domestic water use accounts for _____ percent of all water used in the United States.
(a) 1; (b) 10; (c) 50; (d) 90; (e) 99.

3. Electric power generating plants account for _____ percent of all water used in the United States.
(a) 7; (b) 23; (c) 38; (d) 69; (e) 93.

4. Agriculture accounts for _____ percent of all water used in the United States.
(a) 9; (b) 20; (c) 41; (d) 76; (e) 88.

5. Dams provide a net _____ of water and a _____ controlled flow of the stream.
(a) gain, more; (b) loss, less; (c) gain, less; (d) loss, more.

6. If the present pattern of water use continues, wells in the Ogallala aquifer beneath the high plains will
(a) never dry up; (b) dry up early in the next century; (c) dry up early next year; (d) increase in water content.

7. Subsidence of the Earth's surface
(a) can be caused by removal of ground water; (b) can be caused by excessive addition of irrigation water; (c) results from expansion of the pore spaces in an aquifer; (d) can usually be reversed.

8. An example of non-point source of pollution is
(a) a septic tank; (b) a gasoline spill; (c) a factory; (d) fertilizer spread over a farmer's field; (e) all of the above.

9. Which is the most logical sequence of steps in identifying and treating a contaminated aquifer?
(a) discovery, eliminating the source, monitoring, modeling, remediation (b) eliminating the source, monitoring, discovery, modeling, remediation (c) remediation, monitoring, eliminating the source, discovery, modeling (d) modeling, monitoring, discovery, remediation, eliminating the source

10. The pollution of Love Canal was caused by
(a) biodegradable wastes; (b) plant nutrients; (c) industrial organic compounds; (d) disease organisms; (e) radioactive materials; (f) sewage.

11. Sewage contains a high concentration of
(a) radioactive materials; (b) nonbiodegradable pollutants; (c) industrial organic compounds; (d) disease organisms; (e) toxic inorganic compounds.

12. Organochloride pesticides are troublesome water pollutants because they are
(a) radioactive materials; (b) nonbiodegradable pollutants; (c) plant nutrients; (d) disease organisms; (e) toxic inorganic compounds.

13. The oxygen that fish use in respiration comes from
(a) air dissolved in water; (b) the oxygen atoms in water molecules; (c) the oxygen content of the food they eat; (d) the oxygen in air that fish obtain when they jump out of the water; (e) the oxygen in phosphates.

14. Which of the following is not a problem in ground water pollution?
(a) Sewage pollutes water in wells. (b) Industrial wastes contaminate water in wells. (c) Plant nutrients cause algal blooms. (d) Gasoline from underground tanks seeps into rock and soil.

15. The only feasible method for disposal of radioactive wastes is
(a) dispersal; (b) destruction; (c) isolation; (d) recycling.

16. During the first twenty-five years of the Clean Water Act the total discharge of pollutants into the nations waters has _____.
(a) increased; (b) decreased; (c) remained unchanged; (d) ended completely.

True or False:

1. Most irrigation water is withdrawn, but not consumed.

2. Dams and reservoirs result in a net loss of surface water.

3. Streams erode their beds and banks more rapidly below a dam than if the dam didn't exist.

4. Sediment does not accumulate in a reservoir above a dam because the water in the reservoir continues to flow.

5. Salt water intrusion occurs when excessive pumping of fresh ground water occurs in a coastal area.

6. The problems that occurred at Love Canal in New York are an example of ground water pollution.

7. The 1972 Clean Water Act stated that by 1985 the discharge of pollutants into navigable waters should be eliminated.

8. The Superfund provides an emergency fund to clean up hazardous waste sites.

9. Arsenic is an example of an industrial organic compound.

10. Forty percent of the fresh water in the United States is unsafe for human use.

11..More than 50 percent of the people in the United States drink ground water.

12. Ground water in rural areas is generally pure because there are no factory discharges.

13. Radioactive wastes can be disposed of by incineration, but the process is expensive and prone to emitting dangerous pollutants.

14. The DOE defines a permanent repository as one that will isolate radioactive wastes for 100,000 years.

Completion:

1. Any process that uses water, and then returns it to the Earth locally is called _____.

2. A process that uses water, and then returns it to the Earth far from its source is called
_____.

3. If water is withdrawn faster than it can flow into a well a/an _____ _____ _____ forms
near the well.

4. Excessive removal of ground water can cause _____, the sinking or settling of the Earth's
surface.

5. _____ _____ _____ compares the cost of pollution control with the cost of
externalities.

6. _____ is a technique that uses microorganisms to decompose a contaminant in ground
water.

7. The Comprehensive Environmental Response, Compensation, and Liability Act is commonly
known as _____ and abbreviated as _____.

8. Of the 8 types of pollutants, DDT is an example of a _____ _____.

9. Of the 8 types of pollutants, plutonium is an example of a _____.

10. After all the oxygen in a waterway is consumed, _____ _____ take(s) over.

Answers for Chapter 20:

Multiple Choice:
1. b; 2. b; 3. c; 4. c; 5. d; 6. b; 7. a; 8. d; 9. a; 10. c; 11. d; 12. b; 13. a; 14. c; 15. c; 16. b

True or False:
1. F; 2. T; 3. T; 4. F; 5. T; 6. T; 7. T; 8. T; 9. F; 10. T; 11. T; 12. F; 13. F; 14. F.

Completion:
1. withdrawal; 2. consumption; 3. cone of depression; 4. subsidence; 5. Cost benefit analysis; 6. Bioremediation; 7. Superfund, CERCLA; 8. industrial organic compound; 9. radioactive material; 10. anaerobic bacteria.

CHAPTER 21

Geologic Resources

Discussion

In this chapter we describe the nature, origin, and reserves of geologic resources, which fall into two categories: mineral resources and energy resources. Mineral resources include all useful rocks and minerals, and occur as nonmetallic resources and metals. Energy resources occur as fossil fuels, nuclear fuels, and alternative energy resources.

In the first portion of the chapter, we describe the nature of ore and mineral reserves, and then describe the geologic processes and environments in which ore forms. In Section 21.3 we discuss the scientific, economic, and geopolitical factors that change total mineral reserves and the availability of metals and other geologic commodities. In Section 21.4, we describe the origin, mining, and reserves of coal, then in Section 21.5 we discuss mining, refining, and smelting of metals and coal, including environmental aspects of these processes. Starting with Section 21.6, we describe the nature, origin, economics, environmental aspects, and geopolitics of petroleum, nuclear fuels, and alternative energy resources. We describe how conservation can function as the most efficient and least expensive alternative energy resource. A Focus On box describes the 1872 Mining Law and its effects on public land in the United States.

Answers to Discussion Questions

1. Metal reserves will last longer if we discover new ore bodies, develop technology to mine and refine low-grade ores more cheaply and thus increase known reserves, recycle existing materials, or consume fewer metals. Rapid consumption and a throw-away society lead to more rapid depletion.

2. Some elements are quite similar in chemical behavior to other elements. This is particularly true of those that are close together in the Periodic Table. If two or more similar metals are present, they commonly dissolve in solutions, and then precipitate together. Thus, a single ore deposit may contain two or more valuable metals. For example, silver is chemically similar to lead, and silver is commonly found in galena, the principle ore of lead. In fact, many galena deposits are mined not for lead, but for the silver. Copper, lead, and zinc are commonly associated in the same mineral deposit. The manganese nodules of the deep sea floor are typically rich in iron, nickel, cobalt, and other similar metals.

3. Each student will have a different answer to this question. It is raised to increase awareness of our dependence on our resource base and to provide a springboard for discussion of recycling and conservation.

4. Sedimentary rock for reasons discussed in the text.

5. You would first look for signs of past life. If you found such signs, you would look for rocks similar to those bearing fossil fuels on Earth, or for similar structures that might have trapped, or otherwise preserved fossil fuels.

6. No, coal is a nonvolatile solid. It won't flow or evaporate and therefore it doesn't escape.

7. Problems involved in predicting fossil fuel reserves include uncertainties about the quantity of undiscovered reserves, uncertainties about predicting consumption rates, and uncertainties about the technologies and economics of mainstreaming secondary and tertiary recovery methods, tar sands, oil shales, and similar fossil fuel reserves. In addition, alterations in use patterns of alternative energy resources based on economic and technological changes could radically effect consumption rates of fossil fuels. Uncertainties about the accessibility of global reserves are based on political instability in several major oil-exporting nations.

8. Elements are never consumed, they are just dispersed so that it becomes expensive, sometimes prohibitively so, to collect them once again. If rates of recycling increase, the life-span of metal reserves can be extended. Fossil fuels represent stored chemical potential energy and when they are burned, this potential is lost. The Second Law of Thermodynamics assures us that this energy cannot be recovered and reused to produce work and heat.

9. This discussion can go on for a very long time, because so many of our current environmental problems, global economics, and international politics are directly related to energy resources.

An economically-viable solar cell that could be installed in individual homes, businesses, and industry would greatly diminish or eliminate the need for dams, coal-fired generating plants, nuclear reactors, and power companies. At the same time, environmental impacts of these traditional electricity generation systems would also diminish.

So much money is invested in power companies that development of a cheap solar cell would alter economic balances, shifting money from conventional fossil fuel and power production to solar cell production. Small investors and huge corporations would suffer losses. The complexion of international trade would change, as oil and coal prices would respond to diminished demand. The changes would have important political ramifications, as tiny but politically powerful oil-producing nations would lose influence, and nations that produce solar cells would gain it.

10. Solar energy warms the Earth's surface unevenly, creating wind. The Sun's heat is the major cause of evaporation of water from the Earth's surface, which drives the water cycle and causes streams to flow. Dams harness the energy of the flowing water. Winds drive sea waves.

Selected Reading

General references on formation of ore deposits are:
George Brimhall, "The Genesis of Ores." *Scientific American*, May 1991, p. 84.

Anthony M. Evans, *Introduction to Mineral Exploration.* Cambridge, MA: Blackwell Scientific Publications, 1995, 420 pages.

Anthony M. Evans, *Ore Geology and Industrial Minerals, An Introduction, Third Edition.* Cambridge, MA: Blackwell Scientific Publications, 1992, 400 pages.

Peter Harben "Strategic Minerals." *Earth*, July 1992. p. 36.

Jack E. Oliver, The Big Squeeze, How Plate Tectonic Redistributes Mineral and Organic Resources." *The Sciences*, July/August 1991.

K. L. Von Damm, "Seafloor Hydrothermal Activity: Black Smoker Chemistry and Chimneys." *Annual Review of Earth and Planetary Sciences 18*(173), 1990.

The global environmental impact of mining is discussed in:
Earle A. Ripley, Robert E. Redmann, and Adele A Crowder, *Environmental Effects of Mining.* Delray Beach, FL: St. Lucie Press, 1996, 356 pages.

John E. Young, *Mining the Earth.* Washington, D.C.: Worldwatch Press, 1992, 53 pages.

Two references on the 1872 mining law in the United States are
Richard E. Blubaugh "1872 Mining Law: Time for Clarification and Affirmation." *Geotimes*, April 1992, p. 6.

Robert F. Burford, "The Mining Law of 1872." *Geotimes*, March 1990, p. 16.

Fossil fuels and global energy are discussed in:
Norbert Berkowitz, *An Introduction to Coal Technology*. San Diego: Academic Press, 1993, 386 pages.

William Fulkerson, Roddie R. Judkins, and Manoj K. Sanghvi, "Energy From Fossil Fuels." *Scientific American*, September 1990, p. 129.

John Gever, Robert Kaufman, David Skole, and Charles Vorosmarty, *Beyond Oil*. Boulder: University of Colorado Press, 1991, 351 pages.

Harold M. Hubbard, "The Real Cost of Energy." *Scientific American*, April 1991.

Thomas H. Lee, Ben C. Ball, Jr., and Richard D. Tabors, *Energy Aftermath*. Boston: Harvard Business School Press, 1990, 274 pages.

Two references on nuclear energy and its consequences are:
Robin Herman, *Fusion: The Search for Endless Energy*. New York: Cambridge University Press, 1990, 267 pages.

Grigori Medvedev, *No Breathing Room: The Aftermath of Chernobyl*. New York: Basic Books, 1993, 213 pages.

The politics of ore deposits:
Lawrence J. MacDonnell, *Natural Resources Policy and Law: Trends and Directions*. Cambridge, MA: Harvard University Press, 1993, 241 pages.

Data on energy supply and demand are from:
http://www.eia.doe.gov

Thousands of books have been written recently on conservation and alternative energy sources. Two of our favorites are:
Christopher Flavin and Nicholas Lenssen, *Beyond the Petroleum Age*. Washington, DC: Worldwatch, 1990. 65 pp.

Scientific American, *Energy For Planet Earth*. San Francisco: W.H. Freeman, 1991. 161 pp.

Chapter 21 Test

Multiple Choice:

1. Ore is
(a) any concentration of metals; (b) a concentration of metals that can be mined profitably; (c) a concentration of fossil fuels; (d) a concentration of nonmetallic resources.

2. Fossil fuels are
(a) renewable; (b) formed from the remains of plants and animals; (c) found mainly in igneous rocks; (d) quarried from of limestone (e) being formed as rapidly as they are being consumed.

3. Crystal settling occurs
(a) whenever metal-bearing solutions encounter changing conditions that cause precipitation; (b) when early formed crystals sink to the bottom of a magma chamber; (c) when surface streams slow down and deposit sediment; (d) when the lightest crystals rise to the top of a magma chamber.

4. Hydrothermal processes
(a) form relatively little ore; (b) form more ore than any other process; (c) form most sand and gravel deposits; (d) form coal and oil.

5. Large, low grade hydrothermal ore deposits are
(a) hydrothermal vein deposits; (b) pegmatites; (c) layered mafic deposits; (d) placer deposits; (e) disseminated ore deposits.

6. Evaporite deposits form
(a) by precipitation from water; (b) as magma solidifies; (c) by sedimentary sorting; (d) by hydrothermal solutions.

7. Placer ore deposits form
(a) whenever metal-bearing solutions encounter changing conditions that cause precipitation; (b) when magma cools slowly deep underground; (c) when streams or waves sort sediment according to density; (d) when landlocked lakes dry up; (e) when the oxygen content of the atmosphere changed.

8. Most of the world's iron is mined from
(a) banded-iron formations; (b) marine evaporites; (c) placer deposits; (d) disseminated ore deposits; (e) gold.

9. Coal reserves are thought to be sufficient to last
(a) a few years; (b) a few decades; (c) a few centuries; (d) forever, because coal forms faster than we use it.

10. Coal forms
(a) when buried peat loses most of its hydrogen and oxygen; (b) when buried peat loses most of its hydrogen and carbon; (c) from the remains of marine microorganisms; (d) from banded iron formations.

11. _____ releases no sulfur when burned, has a higher net energy yield than other fossil fuels, and can be extracted and used without refining.
(a) Coal (b) Natural gas (c) Propane (d) Petroleum.

12. Mud converts to shale and organic material converts to liquid petroleum
(a) when pressure and temperature are increased due to burial under younger sediment; (b) very quickly in the ocean; (c) when pressure and temperature are decreased by burial under younger sediment; (d) in the range of 0 to 30°C.

13. The source rock for most oil is
(a) granite; (b) banded-iron formations; (c) shale; (d) limestone; (e) peat.

14. To form an oil reservoir, cap rocks must be
(a) porous; (b) permeable; (c) impermeable; (d) thick; (e) thin.

15. An oil reservoir is most similar to
(a) an underground pool or lake; (b) a thick deposit of tar; (c) an oil-soaked sponge; (d) kerogen saturated shale.

16. Tar sands are permeated with
(a) kerogen; (b) peat; (c) bitumen; (d) natural gas.

17. Low-grade oil shales
(a) require more energy to mine and convert the kerogen to petroleum than is generated by burning the oil; (b) will become profitable to mine if the price of oil rises; (c) can be pumped if

detergents are added to the reservoir; (d) are currently being used for fuel.

18. Electricity generated by nuclear power is _____ expensive than that generated by coal-fired power plants.
(a) more (b) less (c) about equally

19. The major fuel in nuclear power plants is an isotope of
(a) strontium (b) uranium (c) thorium (d) plutonium (e) sulfur.

20. Alternative energy sources
(a) are nonrenewable; (b) are renewable; (c) have the potential to supply only a small fraction of our energy needs; (d) are usually more polluting than nuclear fuels.

True or False:

1. More money has been made mining sand and gravel than gold.

2. Placer deposits form by crystal settling.

3. Several times during the history of the Earth, shallow seas covered large portions of North America and precipitated evaporite deposits.

4. Bauxite is an example of a hydrothermal deposit.

5. Pure metallic iron is common in the Earth's crust.

6. Plant matter is composed mainly of carbon, hydrogen, and oxygen.

7. If conditions are favorable, petroleum is forced out of the source rock and migrates to a nearby layer of sandstone or limestone to accumulate in a reservoir.

8. Crude oil is a gooey, viscous, dark liquid made up of thousands of different chemical compounds.

9. Coal is forming today in some swamps.

10. Coal can be used directly in conventional automobiles.

11. On the average, more than half of the oil in a reservoir is left behind after a well has "gone dry."

12. Small quantities of sulfur are present in coal.

13. In a breeder reactor, U-238 is converted to Pu-239, an isotope of plutonium that is fissionable.

14. In 1990, the US. was an oil exporting nation.

15. A solar cell produces electricity directly from sunlight.

Completion:

1. _____ is any rock sufficiently enriched in one or more minerals to be mined profitably.

2. A corrosive mixture of hot water and dissolved ions is called a/an _____ _____.

3. A/an _____ _____ deposit forms when hydrothermal solutions flow through a large volume of country rock to form an ore deposit with low metal concentration.

4. Table salt and borax form in _____ deposits.

5. Layers of iron-rich minerals sandwiched between beds of silica minerals are called _____ _____ _____.

6. Insoluble ions are left behind by weathering to form _____ deposits.

7. Petroleum, coal, and natural gas are called _____ _____ because they formed from the remains of plants and animals that lived in the geologic past.

8. _____ is a combustible rock composed mainly of carbon.

9. A/an _____ _____ is any barrier to the upward migration of oil or gas.

10. Tar sands are permeated with a heavy oil-like substance called _____.

11. A waxy, solid organic substance that is the precursor of liquid petroleum is called
_____.

12. Rich offshore oil reserves exist on _____ _____ in many parts of the world,
including the coast of southern California, the Gulf of Mexico, and the North Sea in Europe.

13. Crude petroleum must be _____ to produce gasoline, propane, diesel fuel, motor oil, and
chemicals.

14. A modern nuclear power plant uses a process of radioactivity called _____ to
produce heat and generate electricity.

15. A/an _____ solution involves switching to more efficient implements to save energy.

Answers for Chapter 21

Multiple Choice: 1. b; 2. b; 3. b; 4. b; 5. e; 6. a; 7. c; 8. a; 9. c; 10. a; 11. b; 12. a; 13. c; 14. c; 15. c; 16. c; 17. a; 18. a; 19. b; 20. b

True or False: 1. T; 2. F; 3. T; 4. F; 5. F; 6. T; 7. T; 8. T; 9. T; 10. F; 11. T; 12. T; 13. T; 14. F; 15. T

Completion: 1. Ore; 2. Hydrothermal solution; 3. disseminated ore; 4. evaporite; 5. banded iron formations; 6. residual; 7. fossil fuels; 8. Coal; 9. oil trap; 10. bitumen; 11. kerogen; 12. continental shelves; 13. refined; 14. fission; 15. technical

CHAPTER 22

Motion in the Heavens

Discussion

Astronomers study objects so far away that they can never sample them directly. Cosmologists deduce events that occurred billions of years before the formation of the Earth, at the very instant when space and time were created. Thus our knowledge of the heavens cannot be derived by direct sampling. Rather it is accumulated by interpretation of data to build inferences about events and objects outside the realm of direct experience.

The first great astronomical problem was to explain the motion of the Earth, Sun, planets, and stars --a task so difficult and so compelling that it became a central issue of scientific debate from Aristotle to Newton. In fact, the drive to understand motion in the heavens forced people to alter their patterns of reasoning and became the foundation of modern science.

In this chapter we explain Aristotle's geocentric Universe and trace the evolution of thought to Galileo's heliocentric Solar System. We then explain how Galileo's conclusions were supported by Newton's laws of gravity. With this background, we review the modern understanding of the motions in the Solar System -- planetary motion, the motion of the Moon, and eclipses. Finally, as an introduction to the two following chapters, we introduce the techniques of modern astronomy.

Chapter 22 contains a short Focus On: "The Constellations."

Answers to Discussion Questions

1. (a) rotation on its axis; (b) revolution around the Sun; (c) rotation on its axis.

2. (a) the Earth's rotation; (b) both the Earth's rotation and the Moon's revolution; (c) the Moon's revolution.

3. Aristotle's conclusions were based both on observation and dogma. No modern editor would accept a theory based on the belief that celestial spheres are an expression of God's will. However, Aristotle also reasoned that if the Earth revolved around the Sun, then he should observe a stellar parallax shift. Since he couldn't observe a shift because precise instruments weren't available, he reasoned that the Earth must be stationary. Such reasoning was perfectly logical given the data. Therefore if you were a journal editor in ancient Greece, this line of reasoning would be valid.

4. Older style speedometers consist of a flat plate with numbers printed on it and a moving needle. In most cars the needle is positioned above the number plate. Let us say that the car is moving at 80 km/hr. The driver, looking directly at the instrument, sees the needle in line with the 80 km/hr reading. But the passenger sees the instrument at an angle and according to his line of sight, the needle appears to lie over the 70 km/hr mark. This misreading is the parallax error. Point out to the student that on scientific instruments, there is often a mirror behind the indicator needle. If the observer lines up the needle and the mirror, no parallax error can occur.

5. It would be easier to estimate the distance to nearby stars. The parallax angle is greatest when the observer moves an appreciable distance compared to the distance to the object being studied. Since the diameter of the Earth's orbit is small compared to the distance to even the nearest stars, the angles measured are a very small fraction of a degree. The angles become so small for distant objects that they become impossible to measure.

6. There would be an eclipse of the Sun every new Moon and an eclipse of the Moon every full moon.

7. There are approximately 29 1/2 days in a lunar month and therefore a 12 month lunar year is shorter than a solar year. In some medieval European societies the time difference between the two calendars was considered to be a blank time, and these days were set aside as a winter festival.

Selected Reading

Refer to these excellent standard texts:
Andrew Fraknoi, David Morrison, and Sidney Wolff, *Voyages through the Universe*, Philadelphia: Saunders College Publishing, 1997, 550 pages.

David Morrison, Sidney Wolff, and Andrew Fraknoi, *Abell's Exploration of the Universe 7th ed.* Philadelphia: Saunders College Publishing, 1995, 669 pages.

Jay M. Pasachoff, *Astronomy: From the Earth to the Universe, 5th ed.* Philadelphia: Saunders College Publishing, 1998, 643 pages.

Chapter 22 Test

Multiple Choice:

1. If we knew that the Sun rose every morning in the east and set every evening in the west, approximately 12 hours later, but we had no other information, which of the following conclusions would be reasonable?
(a) The Sun orbits around the Earth once every 24 hours. (b) The Sun orbits around the Earth once every 365 days. (c) The Earth orbits around the Sun once every 365 days. (d) The Earth rotates on its axis once every 365 days.

2. In the Northern Hemisphere, the Pole Star
(a) remains motionless in the sky and all other stars appear to revolve around it; (b) circles the sky relative to the other stars; (c) disappears completely every 29.5 days; (d) appears in the summer and is invisible during the winter months.

3. The model that we use to describe the motion of the heavenly bodies
(a) is the geocentric model; (b) the heliocentric model; (c) states that a sequence of celestial spheres surround the Earth; (d) states that the Earth reverses direction in its orbit, in a process called retrograde motion.

4. Kepler calculated that the planets move in
(a) circular orbits; (b) angular orbits; (c) elliptical orbits; (d) parallax orbits.

5. The reason that planets move in orbits rather than flying off into space in straight lines was first explained by
(a) Copernicus; (b) Galileo; (c) Aristotle; (d) Newton; (e) Brahe

6. The Earth spins approximately _____ times for each complete orbit around the Sun.
(a) 29.5; (b) 2; (c) 365; (d) 12; (e) 100.

7. Different stars and constellations are visible during different seasons because
(a) The Sun's revolution around the Earth changes our view of the night sky; (b) The Earth's revolution around the Sun changes our view of the night sky; (c) parallax shows a shift in the relative positions of the stars; (d) the Earth makes one complete rotation on its axis every 24 hours.

8. The constellation Orion is visible from North America during winter but is not seen on summer evenings. Which of the following statements is true?
(a) The stars in Orion pulsate so that they shine brightly for six months and then are dark for six months. (b) Orion is visible from South America during the summer. (c) Orion is visible from the opposite side of the Earth, India, during the summer. (d) Orion cannot be seen during the summer because the Sun is located between Orion and the Earth.

9. The waxing gibbous moon
(a) occurs just after the full Moon; about 3/4 of the Moon is visible; (b) is a thin crescent that forms after the new Moon; (c) is a thin crescent that forms after the full moon; (d) occurs 10 days after a new Moon; about 3/4 of the Moon is visible.

10. When the Earth lies directly between the Sun and Moon it produces a/an
(a) solar eclipse; (b) absorption spectrum; (c) partial eclipse; (d) constellation; (e) lunar eclipse.

11. Which of the following statements about eclipses is true?
(a) A solar eclipse occurs every full moon. (b) A lunar eclipse occurs every full moon. (c) A solar eclipse occurs every new moon. (d) A lunar eclipse occurs every new moon. (e) none of these.

12. As light passes from the hot interior of a star through the cooler outer layers,
(a) some wavelengths are selectively absorbed in the star's outer atmosphere; (b) some wavelengths are selectively reflected in the star's outer atmosphere; (c) all the energy is absorbed; (d) all of the energy is transmitted.

13. Absorption spectra can be used to detect
(a) the chemical composition of a star; (b) temperature and pressures in the core of a star; (c) the mass of a star; (d) the age of a star.

14. If a star is moving away from Earth, the Doppler effect will cause the frequency of the star's light to shift to a _____ frequency, causing a _____ shift.
(a) higher, red; (b) higher, blue; (c) lower, red; (d) lower, blue.

True or False:

1. Constellations appear and disappear with the seasons.

2. Planets sometimes appear to reverse direction in the night sky and drift westward.

3. Ptolemy modified the geocentric model to explain the retrograde motion of the planets.

4. Galileo proposed the geocentric Universe.

5. The geocentric Universe easily explains retrograde motion.

6. Mars actually reverses its orbital direction to preserve the conservation of momentum.

7. A new Moon occurs when the Moon is on the opposite side of the Earth from the Sun.

8. A planet moves in a straight line unless a force is exerted on it.

9. As the Earth rotates, its axis wobbles.

10. We always see the same lunar surface, and the other side was invisible to us until the Space Age.

11. Normally the Moon lies out of the plane of the Earth's orbit around the Sun.

12. On each successive evening the Moon rises about 53 minutes earlier.

13. The Moon does not emit its own light but reflects light from the Sun.

14. More than 99.99 percent of the spectrum is invisible to the naked eye.

15. Astronomers discovered the element helium in the Sun 27 years before it was discovered on Earth.

16. Most large, modern optical telescopes are refracting telescopes.

Completion:

1. Groups of stars that remain in fixed positions to one another are called _____.

2. _____ change position with respect to the stars.

3. Aristotle proposed a _____ Universe.

4. In the geocentric Universe, a series of concentric _____ _____ made of transparent crystal surround the Earth.

5. _____ is the apparent change in position of an object due to the change in position of the observer.

6. _____ first proposed the heliocentric universe.

7. _____ was the first person to see that the Moon had mountains, hills, craters, and large plains.

8. The _____ _____ Moon appears about four days after a new Moon.

9. _____ was the first person to record dark spots on the Sun.

10. When the Moon passes directly between the Earth and the Sun a/an _____ _____ occurs.

11. The shadow band where the Sun is totally blocked out during a solar eclipse is called the _____.

12. Telescopes that collect light with large curved mirrors are called _____ telescopes.

Answers for Chapter 22

Multiple Choice: 1. a; 2. a; 3. b; 4. c; 5. d; 6. c; 7. b; 8. d; 9. d; 10. e; 11. e; 12. a; 13. a; 14. c.

True or False: 1. T; 2. T; 3. T; 4. F; 5. F; 6. F; 7. F; 8. T; 9. T; 10. T; 11. T; 12. F; 13. T; 14. T; 15. T; 16. F.

Completion: 1. constellations; 2. Planets; 3. geocentric; 4. celestial spheres; 5. Parallax; 6. Copernicus; 7. Galileo; 8. waxing crescent; 9. Galileo; 10. solar eclipse; 11. umbra; 12. reflecting

CHAPTER 23

Planets and Their Moons

Discussion

One important point of our study of planetary geology is that all the protoplanets were composed of the same elements in roughly the same proportions. The major differences were the initial masses and distances from the Sun. Today the planets are quite different from one another, and, to our knowledge, only one our Earth, supports life. Thus, initial differences in mass and distance from the Sun caused chemical and physical changes that amplified over time to create very different environments on the planets.

When we study the tectonics and atmospheric compositions of the planets, and especially of the terrestrial planets, we view the Earth from a new perspective. Students are now familiar with the horizontal tectonics that dominates the geology of our planet. However, when we study Venus and Mars, we see different tectonic environments. The study of these differences is a valuable exercise in scientific thought and teaches the student to think about cause and effect here on Earth. We also learn that the Earth's atmosphere is radically different from that of its neighbors. Partly from our study of neighboring planets, we realize that seemingly small perturbations can alter a planet's atmosphere radically.

Planetary geology is a rapidly changing science because a single spacecraft can alter our view of a planet. Data from Mars Pathfinder and Surveyor spacecraft allowed us to add some of the material on Mars just before the book went to press. At the same time, new spacecraft will add to our understanding of the Solar System while this book is still in use. NASA maintains several excellent websites that can be used to keep up to date in this rapidly changing field.

Answers to Discussion Questions

1. If Mercury rotated more rapidly, daytime temperatures would be cooler and nighttime temperatures would be warmer because surface rock would not have as much time to absorb or radiate heat.

2. The surface of the Earth has been reshaped by tectonics and erosion. As a result, old meteorite craters have been obliterated. Since the Earth and the Moon share the same environment in space, a study of the meteorite craters on the Moon tells us that similar bombardment must have occurred on Earth. In addition, the "genesis rocks" found on the Moon are 4.6 billion years old, while no rocks this old have been found on Earth. Thus, studies of lunar

rocks may provide information about the early history of the Solar System.

3. No, not at all. The greenhouse effect is an amplification process that cannot be readily reversed. If you cooled Venus by $20°C$, the carbon dioxide concentration in the atmosphere would not decrease appreciably and the temperature would probably rise back to its present value.

4. No, the big difference is that Venus has a dense atmosphere that transports heat, while Mercury does not.

5. The surface of Venus is so much hotter than that on Earth that the crust may be more plastic. At the same time, since Venus is smaller than Earth, its mantle is cooler and it has a thicker lithosphere. Thus a mantle plume may distort and fracture surface rocks, creating faults, but be unable to form lithosphere-deep cracks.

6. Venus exhibits tectonic behavior but no horizontal plate motion as explained in question 5, above. In addition, the greenhouse warming of Venus, explained in the text, has led to dramatically different atmospheric and climatic conditions.

7. Scientists first estimate weathering rates in the Venusian atmosphere through laboratory experiments and calculations. Then they compare these estimates with measured mineralogy changes from radar data. This comparison give a relative age determination of the weathered rock as compared with the parent. To determine an absolute date, the age of the parent rock must be known. Because no one has collected Venusian rocks for laboratory analysis, most absolute ages of parent (unweathered rock) are estimated by studying crater abundances.

8. Figure 23-13 shows a giant canyon; Figure 23-14 shows stream deposits. Thus we know that streams have eroded, transported, and deposited sediment. If water existed, we known that the temperature was above freezing and below boiling at some time in the planet's history. But we don't know how long the water flowed across the planet, how much water existed, and what the present conditions are. There are abandoned dry canyons and washes in deserts on Earth, so from these two photos, alone, we can't rule out that water still exists on the planet.

9. (a) If most of the surface is covered by sedimentary rock, weathering must have been significant at some time. We could deduce that there was and perhaps still is ample water and/or an atmosphere to erode rock and transport and deposit sediment. We can deduce that there has been no recent volcanic or tectonic activity to extrude large amounts of lava or to force underlying igneous and metamorphic rocks upward where they would be exposed to form mountain ranges.

(b) The planet is large enough and far enough from the sun to have retained a secondary atmosphere from outgassing and from collisions with comets.

(c) 4.2 to 3.9 billion years ago numerous meteorite showers probably left impact craters on the entire surface of the planet. After this period of bombardment, at least one third and possibly as much as two thirds of the surface was smoothed by lava flows. A second period of meteorite bombardment produced younger, smaller craters within the older ones and in the areas that had been smoothed over. At a later date, tectonic activity built mountain ranges over one third of the planet and obliterated the meteorite craters in this region. The absence of canyons or river channels tells us that there was little or no water on the surface.

10. It is difficult to suggest a plausible scenario to explain how Jupiter would suddenly become a star after 4.6 billion years as a planet. However, Jupiter is the largest planet and its composition is the most star-like. If it had been larger originally, it might have become a star, which is why Mr. Clarke chose Jupiter for his novel.

11. Many of the lighter elements will be blown off the surface of Jupiter, leaving a smaller mass and a larger proportion of heavy elements. Jupiter may become a terrestrial planet.

12. no answer necessary

Selected Reading

An overview of all the planets and their moons is given in:
Ronald Greeley and Raymond Batson, *The NASA Atlas of the Solar System*. New York: Cambridge University Press, 1997.

David Morrison, *Exploring Planetary Worlds*. New York: W. H. Freeman, 1994, 240 pages.

Recent studies of Venus are recounted in:
Peter Cattermore, *Venus: The Geological Story*. Bethesda: UCL/Johns Hopkins Press, 1994, 250 pages.

David Harry Grinspoon, *Venus Revealed: A New Look Below the Clouds of our Mysterious Twin Planet*. New York: Addison-Wesley, 1997, 355 pages.

The exploration and history of the Moon is outlined in:
William David Compton, *Where No Man Has Gone Before: A History of Apollo Lunar*

Exploration Missions. Washington, DC: USGPO, 1990. 415 pp.

Don E Wilhelms, *To a Rocky Moon: A Geologist's History of Lunar Exploration*. Tucson: University of Arizona Press, 1993.

The geology of Mars is discussed in:
William Lowell Putnam, *The Explorers of Mars Hill*. Tucson: University of Arizona Press, 1994, 289 pages.

Michael H. Carr, *Water On Mars*. New York: Oxford University Press, 1996, 229 pages.

Donald Goldsmith, *The Hunt for Life on Mars*. New York: Dutton, 1997, 267 pages.

William Sheehan, *The Planet Mars*. Tempe, AZ: University of Arizona Press, 1996.

A new book on Jupiter is:
Reta Beebe, *Jupiter: The Giant Planet*. Washington: Smithsonian, 1997, 261 pages.

A closer look at the volcanoes of the Solar System is:
Charles Frankel, *Volcanoes of the Solar System*. New York: Cambridge University Press, 1996, 232 pages.

Recent books on comets and comet bombardment are:
Tom Gehrels, *Hazards Due to Comets and Asteroids*. Tempe, AZ: University of Arizona Press, 1995, 1300 pages.

David H. Levy, *Impact Jupiter: The Crash of Comet Shoemaker-Levy 9*. New York: Plenum, 1995, 300 pages.

John S. Lewis, *Rain of Iron and Ice: The Very Real Threat of Comet and Asteroid Bombardment*. New York: Addison-Wesley, 1996, 236 pages.

Fred Schaaf, *Comet of the Century, From Halley to Hale-Bopp*. New York: Springer-Verlag, 1996, 384 pages.

The search for extraterrestrial life is covered in:
Paul Halpren, *The Quest for Alien Planets: Exploring Worlds Outside the Solar System*. New York: Plenum Press, 1997, 293 pages.

Chapter 23 Test

Multiple Choice:

1. The Solar System formed from a
(a) diffuse hot cloud of fusing hydrogen and helium; (b) cold diffuse cloud of dust and gas; (c) hot dense cloud of dust and gas; (d) diffuse hot cloud of fusing hydrogen and helium.

2. Which of the following is not a terrestrial planet?
(a) Pluto; (b) Mars; (c) Earth; (d) Venus; (e) Mercury.

3. Mercury is pockmarked with meteorite craters while the Earth is not because
(a) the Earth is farther from the Sun than Mercury is; (b) meteorites didn't strike the Earth; (c) the Earth's surface was liquid when the great meteorite showers fell; (d) tectonic activity and erosion have obliterated the craters on Earth.

4. The major reason that the surface of Venus is much hotter than that of the Earth is
(a) Venus is still being bombarded by intense meteorite showers; (b) Venus is closer to the Sun than Earth is; (c) the atmosphere of Venus has much more carbon dioxide than Earth has; (d) blob tectonics transmits huge quantities of heat from the Venusian interior to the surface.

5. The Venusian surface
(a) is separated into upland plateaus and deep basalt basins, like the Earth's ocean basins; (b) is entirely covered with meteorite craters; (c) is divided into plates by massive features like the Earth's mid-ocean ridge; (d) contains numerous volcanoes and basalt flows.

6. The Venusian atmosphere is
(a) cold and dense; (b) hot and dense; (c) cold and diffuse; (d) hot and diffuse.

7. The igneous rocks on the Moon tell us
(a) that the Moon has never had meteorite impacts; (b) that the Moon formed when a giant object struck the Earth; (c) that portions of the Moon were once hot and liquid; (d) that the Moon's surface was reshaped by numerous meteorite impacts.

8. The Moon formed
(a) shortly before the Earth; (b) about 4.5 million years ago; (c) about 4.5 billion years ago; (d) about 40 billion years ago.

9. Why was the Moon remained geologically quiet and inactive compared to the Earth?
(a) The Moon is so much larger that it took longer to cool. (b) The Moon is so much smaller that it soon cooled. (c) The Moon has no atmosphere; (d) The lunar crust retained pools of magma.

10. Which of the following statements is not correct about Mars?
(a) Liquid water once flowed across the Martian surface but now Mars is dry. (b) The largest volcano in the Solar System is found on Mars. (c) Ice caps on Mars are mainly frozen carbon dioxide. (d) The surface of Mars contains cratered regions and younger lava plains. (e) The Martian atmosphere is dense with a high concentration of carbon dioxide.

11. The Mars Global Surveyor used its instruments to look for evaporite deposits on Mars. Scientists were interested in looking for these deposits because
(a) evaporite deposits would produce the first evidence that liquid water once flowed across the Martian surface; (b) evaporite deposits would prove that liquid water still flows across the Martian surface; (c) evaporite deposits would show that liquid water existed for a long time on the Martian surface; (d) evaporite deposits would prove that Mars was once covered by a global ocean.

12. The chemical composition of Jupiter is most similar to that of
(a) Mars; (b) the Earth; (c) the Moon; (d) Io; (e) The Sun.

13. Above the surface of Jupiter the atmosphere consists mainly of
(a) liquid metallic hydrogen; (b) liquid hydrogen; (c) oxygen, nitrogen, carbon dioxide, argon, and water; (d) hydrogen, helium, ammonia, methane, water, and hydrogen sulfide.

14. Io has a smooth, nearly crater-free surface because
(a) it has not been bombarded by meteorites; (b) of frequent lava flows; (c) it is not tectonically active; (d) the gravitational effects on Io are slight.

15. The rings of Saturn are believed to be
(a) an auroral display of ionized gases; (b) particles of pure ice; (c) the remains of a hurricane-like storm that was first
recorded by Galileo; (d) small particles of dust, rock, and ice.

16. Both Uranus and Neptune
(a) have atmospheres composed primarily of helium and hydrogen; (b) have interiors composed of liquid metallic hydrogen; (c) can be seen with the naked eye; (d) are less dense than Saturn.

17. Pluto is composed mainly of
(a) a mixture of hydrogen and ice; (b) a mixture of rock and ice; (c) a mixture of rock and hydrogen; (d) a mixture of helium and rock.

18. Which of the following orders of sizes is correct?
(a) Earth > Jupiter > the Moon; (b) Jupiter > the Moon > Earth; (c) Pluto > Saturn > the Moon; (d) Saturn > Mars > Earth; (e) Uranus > Earth > Mercury.

19. The tens of thousands of small orbiting bodies between Mars and Jupiter are called
(a) meteorites; (b) asteroids; (c) comets; (d) meteors.

20. A _____ is composed of ice mixed with bits of silicate rock, metals, and frozen crystals of methane, ammonia, carbon dioxide, carbon monoxide, and other compounds.
(a) meteoroid (b) chondrule (c) comet (d) meteor

True or False:

1. The Jovian planets, Jupiter, Saturn, Uranus, and Neptune lost most of their hydrogen, helium, and other light elements.

2. Mercury orbits the Sun faster than any other planet.

3. Tectonic activity has ceased on Mercury.

4. The atmosphere of Venus is 90 times more dense than the Earth's atmosphere.

5. Venus has mountains higher than Mount Everest.

6. At the present time, the Moon's maria are large oceans of liquid magma.

7. The Moon has a metallic core surrounded by silicate rocks of lower density.

8. The Earth's atmosphere is about twice as dense as that on Mars.

9. Jupiter, Saturn, Uranus, Neptune, and Pluto are all gaseous giants, composed mainly of hydrogen and helium.

10. The Great Red Spot is a huge, hurricane-like storm that has persisted on Jupiter for centuries.

11. Many astronomers suspect that Europa's surface is primarily ice that is floating on liquid water beneath.

12. Saturn would float on water if there were a basin large enough to hold it.

13. Titan's large size and low temperature allow it to have an atmosphere.

14. Pluto has never been visited by spacecraft.

15. Asteroids change their orbits frequently and erratically.

16. Organic molecules have been detected in dust clouds deep in interstellar space.

Completion:

1. Mercury, Venus, Earth, and Mars are mostly solid spheres and are called the _____ _____.

2. The temperature on the sunny side of the planet _____ reaches 450°C, while the shady side is frigidly cold.

3. Venus is much hotter than Earth because of a runaway _____ _____.

4. The lunar maria formed when _____ filled circular meteorite craters.

5. Geologists think that a rising _____ _____ may have formed the Tharsis bulge on Mars.

6. _____ planets have dense gaseous atmospheres, very large liquid interiors, and much smaller solid cores.

7. Jupiter's middle layer, between its core and outer sea of liquid hydrogen, is composed of _____ _____ _____.

8. The rings of Saturn may be the debris of one or more _____ that got too close to the planet.

9. _____ and _____ have magnetic fields titled appreciably from their rotational axis.

10. Europa is a moon of _____.

11. Spacecraft have photographed volcanic eruptions on _____.

12. _____ is the smallest planet in the Solar System.

13. A fallen meteoroid is called a/an _____.

14. Most stony meteorites contain small, round grains about 1 millimeter in diameter called _____, that are composed largely of olivine and pyroxene.

Answers for Chapter 23

Multiple Choice: 1. b; 2. a; 3. d; 4. c; 5. d; 6. b; 7. c; 8. c; 9. b; 10. e; 11. c; 12. e; 13. d; 14. b; 15. d; 16. a; 17. b; 18. e; 19. b; 20. c.

True or False: 1. F; 2. T; 3. T; 4. T; 5. T; 6. F; 7. T; 8. F; 9. F; 10. T; 11. T; 12. T; 13. T; 14. T; 15. T; 16. T.

Completion: 1. terrestrial planets; 2. Mercury; 3. greenhouse effect; 4. lava; 5. mantle plume; 6. Jovian; 7. liquid metallic hydrogen; 8. moons; 9. Uranus and Neptune; 10. Jupiter; 11. Io; 12. Pluto; 13. meteorite; 14. chondrules.

CHAPTER 24

Stars, Space, and Galaxies

Discussion

In this chapter we introduce the structure of our Sun, followed by a description of the life and death of stars. Dying stars produce white dwarfs, neutron stars, or black holes depending on their mass. By about 1970, astronomers understood the fundamental processes that produce energy in a star and that lead a star along its life cycle. H-R diagrams were introduced in 1911 to 1913; astronomers postulated the existence of neutron stars in the 1930s; in 1965 Roger Penrose postulated that a collapsing star could become a black hole; and Jocelyn Bell Burnell discovered pulsars in 1967.

In contrast, until recently, astronomers didn't have the tools to search into deep space with the precision they needed to understand fundamental processes. With the recent launch of the Hubble Space Telescope, the construction of the Keck Telescope, and the launch of numerous deep-space observing satellites, astronomers have made numerous dramatic discoveries concerning the structure and evolution of galaxies and quasars. Armed with this new understanding, they have probed the basic structure and evolution of the Universe.

It is impossible to adequately discuss this complex and exciting field of science in a single chapter. Perhaps this brief introduction will excite some students and motivate them to probe deeper. The references in the bibliography are an excellent place to start.

Answers to Discussion Questions

1. No, sound travels only through matter and cannot travel through the vacuum of space as electromagnetic radiation does.

2. No, Hubble's law applies to galaxies, not stars within the Milky Way. All the galaxies are believed to be flying away from each other, but within a given galaxy stars orbit around the nucleus.

3. The Moon and the planets don't emit light but reflect sunlight; we learn little from studying this reflected light.

4. No, in order to study a distant object as it exists today, information would have to travel faster than the speed of light, which is theoretically impossible.

5. No. The temperature in the Sun is so high that molecules such as H_2, O_2, and H_2O cannot exist. Also, there is little elemental oxygen in the Sun, and finally, ordinary chemical reactions release such small quantities of energy compared with nuclear fusion reactions that their effect would be insignificant.

6. The density of the Sun is regulated by a dynamic balance between the force of gravitation pulling inward and that of radiation pushing outward. The gravitational force diminishes with distance from the core but the radiation remains strong, so the gases are diffuse near the surface of the Sun.

7. blue; red

8. You would know that the star had passed through its hydrogen fusion stage, had probably expanded to become a red giant, contracted again until helium started to fuse, and now the helium fuel was largely consumed. The star would soon experience further drastic changes but the nature of these changes would depend on its mass.

9. A white dwarf is an old, burned out, dense star no longer undergoing fusion. A red giant is still providing energy by fusion. Yes, a star about the mass of the Sun will be a red giant after hydrogen fusion slows down, and will become a white dwarf after the helium is consumed.

10. The star and the planets in a Solar System are initially formed from a single cloud of dust and gas. If that cloud originally contained no heavy elements, any planets would be composed solely of hydrogen and helium. We would not expect life on those planets because life depends on the existence of heavier elements.

11. They are older than our Sun. Our Sun has more heavy elements that are believed to have been formed from the remnants of supernova explosions. Stars with fewer heavy elements originated during an earlier period of galactic and stellar evolution.

12. (a) Stars are too large to emit such a sharp radio pulse, and they cannot possibly rotate so fast. (b) A planet in our Solar System orbits the sun so its position relative to the stars changes continuously. Also, planets do not emit such large quantities of energy. (c) A galaxy is much too large to emit such a sharp radio pulse and cannot possibly rotate so fast. (d) Magnetic storms do not oscillate in a regular, unvarying, periodic manner.

13. If a black hole were a permanent resident in our Solar System, it would distort the orbits of

planets and comets and otherwise perturb the system severely enough to be detected.

14. The best evidence indicates that few black holes exist within the Milky Way's galactic disk and there is a slim chance that a rocket ship would pass into the field of a black hole. Black holes adjacent to stars cause X-ray emissions that provide warning. If a rocket did pass close to one, the craft would be pulled off course by the intense gravitational field. If the navigator was alert enough to notice the problem before the ship fell far into the field, and the rocket engines were sufficiently powerful, the crew could escape unharmed. But it would be a real thriller. We know so little about intergalactic space that it is hard to say -- some theories predict that dark matter is composed of numerous intergalactic black holes.

15. A quasar is much larger than a star, much smaller than a galaxy, and much more energetic than either. As explained in the text, it may be a galaxy in formation.

16. $a < e < d < c < f < b$.

Selected Reading

Stephen Hawking's book sets a space-time reference for this chapter:
Stephen Hawking and Roger Penrose, *The Nature of Space and Time*. Princeton, NJ: Princeton University Press, 1996, 141 pages.

The Hubble telescope has opened new windows in space, recent books on the Hubble findings are:
Daniel Fischer, Sterne und Weltraum, Koniswinter, and Hilmar Duerbeck, *Hubbel, A New Window on the Universe*. New York: Springer-Verlag, 1996, 141 pages.

Carolyn Collins Petersen and John C. Brandt, *Hubble Vision: Astronomy with the Hubble Space Telescope*. New York: Cambridge University Press, 1995, 252 pages.

An interesting new book about our Sun is:
Roger J. Tayler, *The Sun as a Star*. New York: Cambridge University Press, 1996, 256 pages.

Recent titles about black holes are:
Mitchell Begelmen and Martin Rees, *Gravity's Fatal Attraction: Black Holes in the Universe*. New York: W.H. Freeman, 1996, 246 pages.

Michael Hawkins, *Hunting Down the Universe: The Missing Mass, Primordial Black Holes, and Other Dark Matters*. New York: Addison-Wesley, 1997, 278 pages.

Richard Morris, *Cosmic Questions: Galactic Holes, Cold Dark Matter, and the End of Time*. New York: John Wiley and Sons, 1993, 200 pages.

New books about the creation of our Universe are:
Phillip M. Dauber and Richard A. Muller, *The Three Big Bangs: Comet Crashes, Exploding Stars, and the Creation of the Universe*. New York: Addison-Wesley, 1996, 207 pages.

James B. Kaler, *Cosmic Clouds: Birth, Death, and Recycling in the Galaxy*. New York: W.H. Freeman, 1997, 252 pages.

Helge Kragh, *Cosmology and Controversy*. Princeton, N.J.: Princeton University Press, 1996, 501 pages.

Malcolm S. Longair, *Our Evolving Universe*. New York: Cambridge University Press, 1996, 197 pages.

Chapter 24 Test

Multiple Choice:

1. One light year is
(a) the distance between the Earth and the Sun; (b) 9.5 trillion kilometers; (c) 10,000,000 kilometers; (d) 1/3600 of a degree.

2. The Orion absorption nebula
(a) is about as dense as the Earth's atmosphere at sea level; (b) contains all or most of the natural elements; (c) is so hot that its atoms glow like a neon light; (d) is about 100 times as massive as our Solar System.

3. Different regions of the Sun have different temperatures. Which sequence of temperatures is correct, starting with the hottest region first?
(a) core > photosphere > corona; (b) core > corona > photosphere; (c) photosphere > core > corona; (d) corona > core > photosphere.

4. Sunspots are areas
(a) where the temperature is $100°$ cooler than surrounding areas; (b) that appear as towering pillars that rise from the Sun's surface; (c) caused by the Sun's magnetic field restricting heat exchange in the photosphere (d) that generally persist for only a few hours.

5. All main-sequence stars are composed primarily of
(a) hydrogen and helium; (b) hydrogen and oxygen; (c) helium and carbon; (d) hydrogen; (e) helium.

6. The major reason for differences in temperature and luminosities among main-sequence stars is that
(a) some have a higher ratio of hydrogen to helium; (b) some are more massive than others; (c) some are younger than others; (d) some are older than others.

7. When hydrogen fusion ends within the core of a star, the core initially
(a) becomes hotter and expands, (b) becomes cooler and contracts; (c) becomes cooler and expands; (d) becomes hotter and contracts.

8. A red giant

(a) has an extremely hot surface; (b) has an inner core of fusing hydrogen; (c) has an inner core of fusing helium; (e) has an outer shell of fusing hydrogen.

9. A dying star with the mass of our Sun will eventually become a
(a) white dwarf; (b) planetary nebula; (c) supernova; (d) black hole; (e) pulsar.

10. Population I stars are composed of
(a) mostly heavy elements inherited from population II stars; (b) only hydrogen and helium; (c) mostly hydrogen and helium with small amounts of heavy elements; (d) mostly helium with small amounts of hydrogen and smaller amounts of heavy elements.

11. Neutron stars
(a) are dense stars where neutrons are fusing together to form iron; (b) are composed of approximately 75% hydrogen, 24% helium, and 1% other elements; (c) are compressed so tightly that the electrons and protons in the star are squeezed together to form neutrons; (d) are so dense that light cannot escape from them.

12. Black holes are difficult to detect because
(a) they all lie within the cores of massive galaxies and are obscured by clouds of interstellar dust; (b) visible and radio frequency signals emitted from them are weak and erratic; (c) they emit or reflect no light whatsoever; (d) scientists believe that there are only three or four of them in the Universe.

13. What is the diameter of the Milky Way galaxy?
(a) 100,000,000 km; (b) 10 light years; (c) 1,000 light years; (d) 100,000 light years; (e) 10 billion light years.

14. Which statement is <u>not</u> true about the Milky Way galaxy.
(a) The nucleus of the Milky Way may contain a massive black hole. (b) Within the past 100,000 years, a giant explosion occurred near the center of the Milky Way. (c) The nucleus of the Milky Way is obscured by dust and gas. (d) The concentration of stars near outer disk is one million times greater than in the galactic nucleus.

15. Hubble's Law states that
(a) the most distant galaxies are moving toward us at the greatest speeds; (b) the most distant galaxies are moving away from us at the greatest speeds; (c) the closest galaxies are moving toward us at the greatest speeds; (d) the closest galaxies are moving away from us at the greatest speeds.

16. A quasar
(a) releases about as much energy as a normal galaxy even though it is much smaller; (b) releases approximately 100 times as much energy as a large star; (c) releases 10 to 100 times as much energy as an entire galaxy; (d) is much smaller than our Sun.

17. Which is the correct sequence of events that occurred during the evolution of the Universe? (a) Atoms formed, then planets formed, then stars formed, then matter collected into galaxies. (b) Atoms formed, then stars formed, then planets formed, then matter collected into galaxies. (c) Galaxies formed, then atoms formed, then stars formed, the matter collected into planets. (d) Atoms formed, then galaxies formed, then planets formed, then matter collected into stars. (e) Atoms formed, then galaxies formed, then stars formed, then matter collected into planets.

True or False:

1. The sunlight we see from Earth comes from the Sun's core.

2. The stronger gravity in more massive stars makes their hydrogen fusion more rapid and intense.

3. All stars lie in the main sequence.

4. The Sun evolved from a cloud of dust and gas in space and is now midway through its mature phase as a main-sequence star.

5. A red giant is hundreds of times larger than an ordinary star.

6. Five billion years from now, the hydrogen in our Sun's core will be exhausted and the Sun will expand into a red giant.

7. Originally, all the stars in the Universe were composed of nearly pure hydrogen.

8. If you were to shine a flashlight beam, a radar beam, or any kind of radiation at a black hole, the energy would be absorbed.

9. If a star were orbiting a black hole, great masses of gas from the star would be sucked into the black hole, to disappear forever.

10. The Milky Way rotates about its center once every 200 million years, so in the 4.6-billion-year history of the Earth we have completed 23 rotations.

11. The galactic halo and globular clusters are probably remnants of the original proto-galaxy that condensed to form the Milky Way.

12. When we look at close objects we see what is happening now, but when we look at distant objects we see what happened in the past.

Completion:

1. One _____ _____ is the distance traveled by light in a year, 9.5 trillion kilometers.

2. The Sun is composed primarily of hydrogen and _____.

3. The Sun's visible surface is called the _____.

4. Jets of gas called _____ shoot upward from the chromosphere, looking like flames from a burning log.

5. During a full solar eclipse the _____ appears as a halo around the Sun.

6. The _____ _____ of a star is its brightness as seen from Earth.

7. A graph that plots absolute magnitudes versus temperatures is called a/an _____ diagram.

8. After hydrogen fusion ceases in a star, the core contracts, and the outer shell undergoes hydrogen fusion and expands to become a/an _____ _____.

9. When a star the size of our Sun dies, it will blow a ring of gas called a/an _____ _____ into space.

10. The material remaining after the explosion described in question 10 will contract to become a/an _____ _____.

11. When a star between 2 and 3 solar masses dies and explodes, the material left behind after the

explosion condenses to form a/an _____.

12. A small residual star that emits regular, closely spaced electromagnetic signals is a/an_____.

13. A/an _____ is a concentration of billions of stars held together by their mutual gravitation.

14. Large clouds of dust and gas, called _____, exist between the stars in a galaxy.

15. _____ _____ are the most common bright galaxies in our region of the Universe.

16. A spherical _____ _____ of dust and gas surrounds the Milky Way's galactic disk.

17. A/an _____ is smaller than a galaxy, emits more energy, and usually exhibits a large red shift.

Answers for Chapter 24

Multiple Choice: 1. b; 2. b; 3. b; 4. c; 5. a; 6. b; 7. d; 8. e; 9. a; 10. c; 11. c; 12. c; 13. d; 14. d; 15. b; 16. c; 17. e.

True or False: 1. F; 2. T; 3. F; 4. T; 5. T; 6. T; 7. T; 8. T; 9. T; 10. T; 11. T; 12. T.

Completion: 1. light year; 2. helium; 3. photosphere; 4. spicules; 5. corona; 6. apparent magnitude; 7. Hertzsprung-Russell; 8. red giant; 9. planetary nebula; 10. white dwarf; 11. neutron star; 12. pulsar; 13. galaxy; 14. nebulae; 15. Spiral galaxies; 16. galactic halo; 17. quasar.